EAT HEALTHY, EAT HEARTY!

Serve yourself and your family vibrant health and hearty fare as you dine on

◆ Dilled Stuffed Snow Peas
◆ Your Favorite Pasta with Spicy Sausage Bolognese
◆ Light Clam Chowder, New England Style
◆ Belgian Beef and Onion Stew
◆ "Buffalo" Chicken Breasts
◆ Cajun Crab Cakes
◆ Roasted Baby Root Vegetables

Whoever would dream of Profiteroles with Chocolate Sauce in a low-calorie cookbook? They're here, along with treats to tempt the most jaded palate. Yes, you can have your Ricotta Cheesecake with Fresh Raspberry Sauce and eat it too . . . in Corinne T. Netzer's

101 LOW CALORIE RECIPES

101 LOW CALORIE RECIPES

THE
CORINNE T. NETZER
GOOD EATING SERIES

▶ ▶ ▶ ▶ ▶ ▶ ▶ ▶ ▶ ▶

101 LOW
CALORIE
RECIPES

◆ ◆ ◆ ◆ ◆

Corinne T. Netzer

A Dell Trade Paperback

A DELL TRADE PAPERBACK

Published by
Dell Publishing
a division of
Bantam Doubleday Dell Publishing Group, Inc.
666 Fifth Avenue
New York, New York 10103

Book designed by Rhea Braunstein

Illustrated by Alice Sorensen

Cover photo: Pizza with Goat Cheese, p. 45

ISBN: 0-440-50416-3

Printed in the United States of America
Published simultaneously in Canada
March 1993
10 9 8 7 6 5 4 3 2 1

HCR

CONTENTS

INTRODUCTION

101 Low Calorie Recipes is one of five books that comprise my Good Eating series of cookbooks. (The other books are *101 Low Fat Recipes, 101 Low Cholesterol Recipes, 101 Low Sodium Recipes,* and *101 High Fiber Recipes.*)

While the calories are greatly reduced in these recipes, the taste is still way up there, enabling you to go on your diet and maintain your weight without making the usual sacrifices. Unlike most diet fare, the dishes in this book are varied and flavorful. Although the main thrust here is on dishes that are low in calories, attention has also been paid to overall health values.

You will find recipes here for complete meals—from soup to dessert—and dishes to serve every taste, whether homey or exotic. And because dieting usually means counting calories, I have included the caloric content of each dish. These calculations are based on the latest data from the United States Department of Agriculture and information obtained from various food producers and processors.

Enjoy!

C.T.N.

SAUCES
and
DRESSINGS

◆ ◆ ◆ ◆ ◆

ARUGULA PESTO
WITH WALNUTS

▶ ▶

You'll find this pesto a refreshing alternative to the usual basil-pignoli combination.

Spoon the sauce over pasta, meat, or poultry. Or try it with my Hearty Minestrone (page 37)—spread it on thin slices of toasted Italian bread, place the bread in individual soup bowls, and ladle in the soup.

 1 *cup tightly packed arugula leaves, trimmed, rinsed, and drained*
 1/4 *cup tightly packed Italian flat leaf parsley, trimmed, rinsed, and drained*
 2 *large cloves garlic, coarsely chopped*
 2 *teaspoons fresh lemon juice*
 2 *tablespoons chopped walnuts*
 1 *tablespoon olive oil*
    Salt and freshly ground pepper to taste
 2 *tablespoons freshly grated Parmesan cheese*

1. Place arugula, parsley, garlic, lemon juice, and walnuts in food processor. Process, scraping down sides as necessary, until ingredients are finely pureed.

2. Add oil and process until mixture is smooth and thoroughly blended. If necessary, add additional lemon juice, taste, and add salt and pepper, if desired. (At this point, the pesto can be refrigerated or frozen for future use.)

3. If you are using the pesto immediately, add cheese and process briefly.

MAKES ABOUT ³/₄ CUP
APPROXIMATELY 25 CALORIES PER TABLESPOON

◆◆◆◆◆

ROASTED RED PEPPER PUREE

▶▶▶▶▶▶▶▶▶▶▶▶▶▶▶▶▶▶▶▶▶▶▶▶▶▶▶

Excellent with grilled or broiled fish or as a base for a pasta sauce.

2   *large red bell peppers, roasted, or 1 cup water-packed roasted peppers, drained*
2   *teaspoons olive oil*
2   *tablespoons red wine vinegar*
2   *tablespoons chopped fresh parsley*
     Salt and freshly ground pepper to taste

1. Cut roasted peppers into pieces. (If using fresh peppers, roast them following directions on page 21, steps 1 through 3.)

2. Combine peppers with remaining ingredients in a food processor and process until coarsely pureed or to desired consistency.

MAKES ABOUT 1 CUP
APPROXIMATELY 96 CALORIES PER RECIPE

◆ ◆ ◆ ◆ ◆

UNCOOKED FRESH TOMATO SAUCE

▶ ▶

I rresistible because it has that just-harvested taste, this substantial, all-purpose sauce is a perfect match for pasta or steamed vegetables (especially spinach, broccoli rape, asparagus, or leeks). Spread it on sliced crusty bread as an appetizer; pour it over meat, fish, or poultry loaves; or serve it with grilled fish . . . you name it!

   4   *large ripe tomatoes, finely chopped*
 $^1/_2$ *cup chopped scallions, white and tender greens*
 $^1/_4$ *cup chopped fresh basil or parsley*
   2   *teaspoons olive oil*
   2   *sun-dried tomato halves (not oil-packed), soaked in boiling water until softened, drained, and chopped*
   1   *large clove garlic, pressed or finely minced*
   2   *teaspoons chopped fresh oregano or 1 teaspoon dried*
      Salt and freshly ground pepper to taste

Combine all ingredients and mix thoroughly.

MAKES ABOUT 2$^1/_2$ CUPS
APPROXIMATELY 29 CALORIES PER $^1/_4$ CUP

♦ ♦ ♦ ♦ ♦

JALAPEÑO SALSA

▶ ▶

Serve this sauce over chicken, tacos, and hamburgers. It also makes a jazzy dip and is a terrific condiment for Mexican-style dishes and grilled fish.

	Vegetable oil cooking spray
1	*small onion, finely chopped*
1	*medium clove garlic, minced*
4	*cups peeled, seeded, chopped tomatoes, with juice*
1	*cup low sodium chicken broth*
2	*fresh jalapeño peppers, seeded and minced (wear rubber gloves)*
2	*teaspoons chopped fresh oregano or 1 teaspoon dried*
¼	*teaspoon fresh lemon or lime juice*

1. Coat a nonstick skillet with a thin film of cooking spray. Add onion and garlic and sauté over low heat, stirring frequently, for about 4 minutes or until onion is softened. Add tomatoes, raise heat, and bring to a boil.

2. Reduce heat to medium, add broth, and simmer the mixture for about 6 minutes or until slightly reduced and thickened.

3. Add jalapeños, oregano, and lemon or lime juice and stir to combine ingredients well.

MAKES ABOUT 3 CUPS
APPROXIMATELY 24 CALORIES PER ¼ CUP

◆ ◆ ◆ ◆ ◆

CRANBERRY APPLESAUCE

▶ ▶

Tart and chunky, this delicious sauce is admirable on its own, as a compliment to roasted meats and poultry, or spooned, while still warm, over vanilla ice milk.

During the summer, when berries are at their best, you can substitute strawberries or raspberries for the cranberries (the difference in calories is negligible).

> 3   tart apples, preferably Granny Smith, peeled, cored, and diced
> 2   tablespoons water
> 3/4 cup fresh cranberries, picked over and rinsed
> 1   tablespoon fresh lemon juice
> 1   teaspoon or packet sugar substitute (optional)

1. Combine apples and water in a saucepan, cover and cook over medium-low heat for about 15 minutes, stirring occasionally.

2. Add remaining ingredients, reduce heat to low, cover, and simmer, stirring often, for an additional 15 minutes or until fruit is well cooked. (If there is excess liquid, raise heat, remove cover, and simmer for a few minutes.)

MAKES ABOUT 2 CUPS
APPROXIMATELY 36 CALORIES PER 1/4 CUP

◆ ◆ ◆ ◆ ◆

HORSERADISH APPLESAUCE

▶▶▶▶▶▶▶▶▶▶▶▶▶▶▶▶▶▶▶▶▶▶▶▶▶▶▶

This serendipitous creation was inspired by overwhelming boredom. Tired of the usual mustard, mayonnaise, vinegar coupling with cold chicken, I yanked some of my homemade Cranberry Applesauce from the fridge. Now, cold chicken and applesauce is a lovely combination, indeed. But I wanted some spunk! So, reaching toward the shelf that houses my chutneys, preserves, jalapeño peppers, and such, I retrieved the first container my fingers descended on: prepared horseradish. Mixing a bit of the horseradish with applesauce produced a marriage made in heaven—terrific with any cold roasted meat as well as chicken.

Although my Cranberry Applesauce goes extremely well with the horseradish, any unsweetened applesauce will do nicely.

$1/4$ *cup prepared white horseradish, or more to taste*
1 *cup chilled Cranberry Applesauce (page 8), or other unsweetened applesauce*

Combine horseradish and applesauce and stir until thoroughly blended. Chill for at least 1 hour before serving.

MAKES 1¼ CUPS
APPROXIMATELY 7 CALORIES PER TABLESPOON

◆ ◆ ◆ ◆ ◆

BASIC BÉCHAMEL SAUCE

▶ ▶

In the not-too-distant past, white sauces such as béchamel were the mainstay of French and, to a lesser extent, Italian cuisines. Rich with heavy cream, flour, and butter, these notorious artery-cloggers appeared in all manner of dishes.

By eliminating the heavy cream and butter and reducing the amount of flour, this recipe produces a more than reasonable facsimile with a reassuring nod to a lighter, less oppressively fatty way of eating. Serve in the same way you would the heavyweight version.

By adding ingredients you can enhance the flavor and extend its uses. Add capers and parsley and serve over poached fish or poultry; add tomato sauce, puree, or paste to create a lovely pool in which to place shoestring zucchini, yellow squash, or julienned braised leeks. Variations for Mornay Sauce and Cheddar Cheese Sauce follow.

1¹/₂ tablespoons finely minced onions
2 tablespoons low sodium chicken broth or water
2 tablespoons flour
1 cup low fat (2%) milk
2 tablespoons nonfat dry milk
Salt and white pepper to taste

1. In a medium saucepan, preferably nonstick, braise onions in broth or water until onions are very soft and liquid is evaporated.

2. Sprinkle with flour and stir well to dissolve, then add milk and nonfat dry milk. Cook over medium-low heat, stirring, until thickened. Taste and add salt and pepper, if desired.

MAKES ABOUT 1 CUP
APPROXIMATELY 224 CALORIES PER RECIPE
APPROXIMATELY 14 CALORIES PER TABLESPOON

Mornay Sauce: Elegant over crab, oysters, steamed fillet of sole, turbot, cod, or hake; nifty over macaroni or other short, stubby, tubular pasta.

Add 1 ounce shredded low fat Swiss cheese to the basic recipe and stir over very low heat until cheese is melted and all ingredients are blended. (Add an additional 90 calories per recipe; 6 calories per tablespoon.)

Cheddar Cheese Sauce: Great fun as a heated fondue for dipping skewered toasted bread or apple or pear slices; serve over macaroni or other short pasta; use it to dress up steamed asparagus, Brussels sprouts, cabbage, and so forth.

Add 1 ounce shredded low fat cheddar cheese (and a dash of Worcestershire sauce and 1/2 teaspoon dry mustard, if desired) to the basic recipe and stir over very low heat until cheese is melted and all ingredients are blended. (Add an additional 90 calories per recipe; 6 calories per tablespoon.)

◆ ◆ ◆ ◆ ◆

LIGHT BEARNAISE SAUCE

▶ ▶

𝔸 variation of one of my former heartthrobs (I'm afraid I'm being literal), which is usually made with egg yolks, vinegar, shallots, and a béchamel sauce base. Good with baked, poached, or broiled fish, or very lean meat.

> 1 cup Basic Béchamel Sauce (*page 10*)
> ½ cup dry white wine
> 1 large shallot, minced, or 1½ tablespoons minced onion
> 2 tablespoons chopped fresh tarragon or 2 teaspoons dried
> 1 tablespoon chopped fresh parsley
> 1 tablespoon wine or tarragon vinegar

1. Prepare Basic Béchamel Sauce and keep warm.

2. In a small saucepan, combine wine, shallot or onion, herbs, and vinegar, bring to a boil and simmer for 10 to 15 minutes or until reduced by a little more than half. Cool slightly and stir mixture into warm Basic Béchamel Sauce. Serve warm.

MAKES ABOUT 1¼ CUPS
APPROXIMATELY 13 CALORIES PER TABLESPOON

◆ ◆ ◆ ◆ ◆

BASIC CREAM-STYLE DRESSING

▶▶▶▶▶▶▶▶▶▶▶▶▶▶▶▶▶▶▶▶▶▶▶▶▶▶▶

While my Basic Béchamel Sauce (page 10) serves as the substitute for many of my cream-style cooking sauces, this is the base I use for my creamy dressings and all those tasty condiments that are normally off-limits.

This tofu and yogurt dressing is low in calories, cholesterol, and fat, and takes very well to any number of added ingredients (see the variations that follow or experiment with other additions). On its own, it makes a delightful dressing for a salad of mixed greens, tuna, chicken, or potatoes.

$^1/_4$ *cup plus 2 tablespoons soft silken tofu*
$^1/_4$ *cup low fat plain yogurt*
1   *teaspoon Dijon mustard*
1   *small shallot, finely minced*
$1^1/_2$ *tablespoons fresh lemon juice*
       Salt and freshly ground pepper to taste

Combine all ingredients in a small bowl and stir until well blended. Chill at least 1 hour before serving.

MAKES ABOUT $^3/_4$ CUP

APPROXIMATELY 222 CALORIES PER RECIPE

APPROXIMATELY 19 CALORIES PER TABLESPOON

Tartar Sauce: Stir in 2 tablespoons pickle relish (add 13 calories per recipe; 1 calorie per tablespoon).

Russian Dressing: Stir in 1 tablespoon tomato ketchup or tomato paste (regular or sun-dried) and a small pressed clove garlic (add 17 calories per recipe; 2 calories per tablespoon).

Remoulade Sauce: Add ½ teaspoon dried tarragon, a small pressed clove garlic, and 2 teaspoons drained, rinsed, and chopped capers. Stir until all ingredients are well blended (add 11 calories per recipe; 1 calorie per tablespoon).

Aioli Sauce: Add a large pressed clove garlic and a pinch of cayenne if you like it spicy (add 5 calories per recipe; less than 1 calorie per tablespoon).

APPETIZERS
and
STARTERS

◆ ◆ ◆ ◆

CEYLON CHICKEN WINGS WITH MINT DIPPING SAUCE

► ►

Some of my favorite flavors are blends of the unusual and seductive spices of India. With that in mind, and as a departure from the usual Buffalo wings (which are un-skinned, deep-fried, and served with blue cheese dip), I created these tidbits. Cool them down by dipping into the minted yogurt sauce.

16	chicken wings (about 2 pounds)
1	tablespoon red wine vinegar
3/4	cup fruity white wine
1	small onion, finely minced
2	medium cloves garlic, minced
1 1/2	teaspoons curry powder, or to taste
1/2	teaspoon ground cumin
1/2	teaspoon ground coriander
1/4	teaspoon turmeric
1/2	teaspoon cayenne, or to taste (optional if using hot curry powder)

DIPPING SAUCE

1	cup low fat plain yogurt
3	tablespoons chopped fresh mint or 1 tablespoon dried
1	tablespoon lemon juice
	Salt and freshly ground pepper to taste

1. Cut off wing tips and discard or reserve for another use, carefully remove skin, and cut wings in half at the joint.

2. Combine vinegar, wine, onion, garlic, and spices, stirring well. Pour mixture into a shallow baking dish or large wide bowl and add chicken, tossing to cover all the wing portions with marinade. Cover and refrigerate for at least 1 hour.

3. Preheat oven to 350°F.

4. Arrange chicken wings in one layer on a baking sheet with sides, pour in most of the remaining marinade, cover with foil, and bake for 20 minutes.

5. Prepare dipping sauce while chicken bakes by combining yogurt with mint, lemon juice, and salt and pepper. Cover and refrigerate until wings are ready to serve.

6. Reset oven to broil, remove foil, brush wings with reserved marinade and broil for 3 to 4 minutes or until golden.

7. Arrange wings around a bowl of chilled dipping sauce; serve wings warm or at room temperature.

MAKES 32 PIECES AND 1 CUP SAUCE
APPROXIMATELY 24 CALORIES PER WING SECTION
APPROXIMATELY 5 CALORIES PER 1/2 TABLESPOON SAUCE

♦ ♦ ♦ ♦ ♦

SHERRY LEMON SHRIMP

▶ ▶

The beautifully flavored marinade transforms plain grilled shrimp into an unusual first course. The lemon juice and cider vinegar add a bright, fresh accent, while the lively heat of the hot pepper sauce can easily be adjusted to individual tastes.

> 2   tablespoons lemon juice
> 2   tablespoons dry sherry
>   Dash hot pepper sauce, or to taste
> 2   tablespoons cider vinegar
> 1   teaspoon low sodium soy sauce
>   Freshly ground pepper to taste
> 1   teaspoon vegetable oil
> 2   teaspoons water
> 1   teaspoon dried oregano
> 24 large shrimp, shelled and deveined
> 12 large radicchio or lettuce leaves
> 6   thin lemon slices for garnish

1. Combine lemon juice, sherry, hot pepper sauce, vinegar, soy sauce, a few grindings of pepper, oil, water, and oregano in a shallow baking dish. Add shrimp and toss lightly. Cover and refrigerate for 15 to 30 minutes. Preheat broiler while shrimp marinates.

2. Lay shrimp in a single layer on a baking sheet and broil for about 3 minutes, turn with a spatula, brush with any

reserved marinade, and broil for an additional 3 minutes or until shrimp are just pink all over and cooked through.

3. Divide radicchio or lettuce among 6 plates and top each with four shrimp. Garnish with lemon slices and serve.

SERVES 6

APPROXIMATELY 53 CALORIES PER SERVING

◆ ◆ ◆ ◆ ◆

ROASTED RED PEPPERS

▶ ▶

$\mathbb{F}$reshly roasted sweet red peppers, simply served, are an elegant way to start any meal. Easy to prepare, roasted peppers are a welcome addition to a buffet or an antipasto and can be used in dishes such as Caponata (page 26), or pureed into a flavorful sauce (page 5).

If you don't plan to serve the roasted peppers immediately they can be refrigerated, well covered, for two or three days. Return them to room temperature before serving.

2   *medium red bell peppers*
1   *teaspoon olive oil*
1   *tablespoon balsamic vinegar*
1   *tablespoon capers, rinsed and drained*
    Salt and freshly ground pepper to taste
2   *teaspoons minced fresh basil or parsley*

1. Place peppers under the broiler or atop a heated grill. Roast peppers until skins blacken on one side. Turn and char until the whole pepper is blackened and blistered.

2. Remove from heat and seal peppers in a brown paper bag for 5 minutes or until peppers are cool enough to handle.

3. Working over a strainer set into a bowl, peel away blackened skin using your hands or a sharp knife. Cut peppers in halves or quarters lengthwise, and remove and discard stalk, white ribs, and seeds.

4. Place peppers on serving dishes. Combine any reserved juice from the peppers with oil, vinegar, capers, and
salt and pepper to taste. Blend well and spoon over peppers.
Sprinkle each serving with ½ teaspoon basil or parsley and
serve.

SERVES 4
APPROXIMATELY 24 CALORIES PER SERVING

◆ ◆ ◆ ◆ ◆

SPINACH SCALLION DIP

▶ ▶

This creamy dip is terrific with crisp fresh vegetables on a
crudités platter—and no one will ever guess it contains
tofu.

$^1/_2$	cup soft silken tofu, drained
$1^1/_2$	cups low fat (1%) cottage cheese
3	ounces light cream cheese
2	tablespoons freshly grated Parmesan cheese
2	tablespoons fresh lemon juice
4	scallions, white bulbs only, cut in halves crosswise
$^3/_4$	cup lightly steamed chopped fresh spinach (about 2 cups uncooked), drained
	Salt and freshly ground pepper to taste

1. Combine tofu, cheeses, and lemon juice in the bowl
of a food processor and process until smooth and creamy.

2. Add scallions and process long enough to chop but
not puree. Add spinach and process briefly, just to mix. Taste
and add salt and freshly ground pepper. Chill for 1 hour.

MAKES ABOUT 2½ CUPS
APPROXIMATELY 16 CALORIES PER TABLESPOON

◆ ◆ ◆ ◆ ◆

CLAMS IN WINE BROTH

▶ ▶

Chunks of heated, crusty bread are in order here for mopping up the wine-scented broth of this delicious starter. Served with a salad, this makes a satisfying light meal for two.

1	*teaspoon oil*
2	*small cloves garlic, chopped*
1/4	*teaspoon hot red pepper flakes, or to taste*
3/4	*cup dry white wine*
1/2	*cup low sodium chicken broth*
1	*teaspoon crumbled dried thyme*
	Juice of 1 large lemon
2	*dozen littleneck clams, scrubbed*
2	*tablespoons thinly sliced pimiento*

1. Heat oil in large pot over a medium-low flame. Add garlic and hot pepper, if desired, and sauté for 2 minutes.

2. Raise heat to medium-high, add wine, broth, thyme, and lemon juice. When liquid boils, add clams. Cover and cook just until clams open, shaking pan occasionally. Remove clams from pan as they open and place in warmed serving bowls.

3. Ladle remaining clams (discard any that do not open) and broth into bowls, sprinkle with pimiento, and serve immediately.

SERVES 4

APPROXIMATELY 62 CALORIES PER SERVING

◆ ◆ ◆ ◆ ◆

DILLED STUFFED SNOW PEAS

▶ ▶

A lovely-looking opener that is a refreshing change of pace from the usual crudités/crackers and dip crowd.

> 1/2   cup low fat ricotta cheese
> 1   teaspoon coarse-grained mustard
> 1   tablespoon minced fresh dill or 1/2 tablespoon dried
>   Salt and freshly ground pepper to taste
> 1/4   cup sesame seeds
> 25   fresh snow peas (about 1/4 pound), stemmed, strings removed

1. Combine ricotta, mustard, and dill in a small bowl, season to taste with salt and pepper, and set aside.

2. Sprinkle sesame seeds into a nonstick skillet, heat skillet gently and sauté seeds, shaking pan frequently, until seeds begin to turn golden. Remove seeds from pan and set aside.

3. Using a very sharp knife, slice open pea pods along the straight side. Spoon cheese mixture into pastry bag fitted with a small tip and pipe mixture into cavity of pods.

4. Place sesame seeds in a shallow dish and dip stuffed edge of pea pods into the seeds. Transfer to serving platter and refrigerate until ready to serve.

MAKES 25 APPETIZER SERVINGS
APPROXIMATELY 24 CALORIES PER SERVING

◆ ◆ ◆ ◆ ◆

CAPONATA

▶ ▶

There are numerous versions of this classic Italian appetizer; mine includes roasted red peppers and zesty sundried tomatoes.

1	*medium eggplant (about 1¼ pounds)*
	Vegetable oil cooking spray
1	*teaspoon olive oil*
1	*stalk celery, chopped*
1	*medium onion, chopped*
5	*tablespoons low sodium chicken or beef broth*
1½	*cups clean, sliced fresh mushrooms*
	Salt and freshly ground pepper to taste
2	*sun-dried tomato halves (not oil-packed), soaked in hot water to soften, drained, and chopped*
1	*large, fresh tomato, chopped, with any accumulated juices, or ¾ cup canned chopped, no-salt-added tomatoes, undrained*
1	*medium red bell pepper, roasted* and cut in pieces*
1	*tablespoon capers, rinsed and drained*
⅓	*cup pitted ripe olive halves, rinsed and drained*
1	*teaspoon chopped fresh oregano or ½ teaspoon dried*
1	*teaspoon sugar*

1. Heat oven to 425°F. Raise top rack to the highest level.

2. Rinse eggplant and roast on a baking sheet, turning every 10 minutes, for 1 hour or until eggplant is soft all over (since eggplants vary in shape, some sections may cook faster than others. Err on the side of slightly undercooked if your eggplant has a noticeable wide and a narrow section). Remove from oven and set aside until eggplant is cooled slightly.

3. When eggplant is cool enough to handle, cut off stem, peel, and cut eggplant lengthwise into slices about 1-inch thick. Remove as many seeds as you can (this is usually not difficult as the seeds tend to stick together in rows), and cut eggplant into cubes. Set in a colander to drain.

4. Heat cooking spray and oil in a deep, nonstick skillet and sauté celery and onion over medium heat until onion begins to brown. Add 4 tablespoons broth and cook, stirring occasionally, until liquid is nearly evaporated.

5. Raise heat a little, add mushrooms and sprinkle with salt and pepper, then add sun-dried tomatoes. When mushrooms soften, add remaining broth and eggplant and sauté until lightly golden.

6. Stir in remaining ingredients, cover, and simmer over low heat for 15 minutes or until eggplant is tender. Uncover and cook for about 10 minutes or until mixture is slightly thickened. Serve warm or at room temperature.

SERVES 8
APPROXIMATELY 55 CALORIES PER SERVING

---

* Roasted red peppers packed in water are available at most supermarkets. If you prefer using fresh peppers, see page 21, steps 1 through 3, for instructions on roasting them.

◆ ◆ ◆ ◆ ◆

SALMON TARTARE

▶ ▶

For this appetizer the salmon *must* be absolutely fresh. If your fishmonger can't guarantee its freshness, don't make this dish.

Walnut oil adds a subtle, delicate flavor, but if it is unavailable, olive oil can be substituted.

1/2	*pound absolutely fresh boneless salmon fillets, skin and all visible fat removed*
1	*small red onion, chopped*
2	*tablespoons plus 1 teaspoon walnut oil*
3	*tablespoons capers, rinsed and drained*
1/4	*teaspoon salt, or to taste*
	Freshly ground pepper to taste
1/4	*cup white vinegar*
1	*teaspoon sugar*
1	*small cucumber, peeled and very thinly sliced*
20	*French bread rounds (about half of a 12-ounce baguette)*
2	*tablespoons chopped fresh cilantro or parsley*
1	*large lemon, thinly sliced*

1. Cut salmon in large chunks and process with the steel knife blade in a food processor, pulsing machine on and off, until salmon is coarsely ground.

2. Transfer salmon to a bowl and mix with onion, 2 tablespoons walnut oil, capers, salt if desired, and three or four grindings of pepper. Cover and chill.

3. While salmon chills, whisk vinegar and sugar in a bowl, add cucumber slices and toss to coat well. Chill until ready to serve.

4. At serving time, toast or bake French bread rounds until lightly golden. Drain cucumber slices and arrange on a platter to create a fan or flower, mound salmon tartare in the center, sprinkle with the remaining teaspoon of walnut oil and cilantro and serve with toasted bread and lemon slices.

20 APPETIZER SERVINGS

APPROXIMATELY **57** CALORIES PER SERVING

◆ ◆ ◆ ◆ ◆

TURKEY MEATBALLS
WITH SPICY DIPPING SAUCE

▶ ▶

These meatballs also make a great sandwich stuffer with a dash of the dipping sauce or your favorite condiment.

Vegetable oil cooking spray
³/₄ *pound ground light meat turkey*
¹/₂ *cup dry unseasoned bread crumbs*
 1 *clove garlic, pressed*
 1 *small onion, finely grated*
 1 *small carrot, finely grated*
 1 *tablespoon minced fresh parsley*
    Salt and freshly ground pepper to taste
 2 *egg whites*

SPICY DIPPING SAUCE
³/₄ *cup low sodium tomato sauce*
 1 *tablespoon cider vinegar*
 1 *teaspoon dried oregano*
¹/₄ *teaspoon cayenne, or to taste*

1. Preheat oven to 350°F. Coat a baking sheet lightly with cooking spray and set aside.

2. In a mixing bowl, combine turkey with bread crumbs, garlic, onion, carrot, parsley, and salt and pepper to taste. Mix well. Add egg whites and mix again until ingredients are thoroughly blended.

3. Form turkey mixture into 24 small balls and place on

---

the prepared baking sheet. Bake meatballs in center of oven for 40 minutes or until well browned and cooked through.

4. About 5 minutes before meatballs are done, prepare sauce by combining tomato sauce with vinegar, oregano, and cayenne in a small saucepan and cook until simmering. Transfer sauce to a small serving bowl.

5. Arrange meatballs on a serving platter, pierce each with a toothpick, and serve accompanied with hot dipping sauce.

MAKES 24 MEATBALLS AND ¾ CUP SAUCE
APPROXIMATELY 30 CALORIES PER MEATBALL
APPROXIMATELY 5 CALORIES PER TEASPOON SAUCE

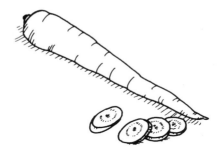

SOUPS
and
CHOWDERS

◆ ◆ ◆ ◆ ◆

TOMATO LEEK SOUP

▶ ▶

The grated Parmesan adds a tasty finishing touch to this superb soup, but if you opt to do without it, you'll save 23 calories per serving.

1	*tablespoon olive oil*
2	*leeks, white and pale greens, well rinsed and chopped*
¹/₂	*medium onion, chopped*
2	*cups low sodium chicken broth*
2	*cups water*
2	*cups coarsely chopped, peeled tomatoes, fresh or canned no-salt-added, juice reserved*
	Pinch dried thyme
	Salt and freshly ground pepper to taste
2	*ounces capellini or angel hair pasta, broken in quarters*
6	*fresh basil leaves, slivered*
	Juice of ¹/₂ large lemon
4	*tablespoons freshly grated Parmesan cheese (optional)*

1. Heat oil in a large pot. Add leeks and onion and sauté over medium-low heat, stirring often, for 10 minutes or until leeks are softened.

2. Raise heat and add broth, water, chopped tomatoes and reserved juice, thyme, and salt and pepper. Bring to a boil, then reduce heat and simmer gently for 30 minutes. If

the soup becomes very thick, add additional water, ¹/₄ cup at a time.

3. Add capellini to pot, stirring so that the pasta doesn't stick together. Cook over medium heat for about 6 minutes or until pasta is tender.

4. Stir in basil and lemon juice. Taste and correct seasonings. Serve in individual heated bowls, sprinkled with grated cheese, if desired.

SERVES 4 GENEROUSLY
APPROXIMATELY 165 CALORIES PER SERVING
APPROXIMATELY 188 CALORIES PER SERVING WITH CHEESE

◆ ◆ ◆ ◆ ◆

HEARTY MINESTRONE

▶ ▶

Show me your minestrone and I can probably tell you what region of Italy it represents. For example, in the southern part of Italy, vegetable soups feature tomatoes, garlic, oil, and more than likely vermicelli or other pasta. The center region favors beans, while the soups prepared in the north will invariably contain rice. Fresh herbs are the hallmark of the minestrone served along the Riviera, and in Rome only the freshest seasonal vegetables and herbs are used. This Good Eating version is really the best of all possible minestrones, with its garlic, beans, macaroni, herbs, spices, and lovely mix of vegetables.

Minestrone is best when hearty and thick. It should never be watery. So, if need be, keep cooking until the liquid is reduced to the desired consistency. On the other hand, if the soup becomes too thick to be a soup, add more broth (at 9 calories per half cup) but don't weaken its flavor by adding water. Minestrone tastes even better the day after it is made and will keep, refrigerated, for two or three days.

To complete this wonderful one-dish meal, just pass around some crusty mixed grain bread.

> 2¹/₂ cups low sodium beef broth or bouillon
> 1 medium onion, chopped
> 1 clove garlic, finely chopped
> 1 cup green cabbage, thinly sliced
> 1 cup peeled, chopped fresh tomatoes

$^1/_2$ cup each: sliced carrots, celery, green beans, and zucchini or yellow squash

$7^1/_2$ ounces canned garbanzo beans, rinsed and drained

$7^1/_2$ ounces canned kidney beans, rinsed and drained

3 cups water

$^1/_2$ teaspoon dried basil

Salt and freshly ground pepper to taste

$^1/_2$ cup uncooked macaroni

4 ounces fresh spinach, well rinsed and shredded (about 2 cups)

1. Heat $^1/_4$ cup broth in a large pot. Add onion, garlic, and cabbage and simmer for 5 minutes or until cabbage softens.

2. Add all remaining ingredients, except macaroni and spinach, and bring to a boil over medium-high heat. Cover, reduce heat, and simmer gently for 15 minutes.

3. Add macaroni and cook for an additional 15 minutes or until vegetables are tender. Add a little water if needed.

4. Stir in spinach and cook until wilted. Transfer to individual heated bowls and serve.

SERVES 6

APPROXIMATELY 145 CALORIES PER SERVING

◆◆◆◆◆

PUREED CARROT SOUP
WITH SHERRY

▶▶▶▶▶▶▶▶▶▶▶▶▶▶▶▶▶▶▶▶▶▶▶▶▶▶▶▶▶

I don't know what your childhood eating experiences were, but mine were filled with those (resented) motherly pearls of wisdom extolling the many virtues of food. "Eat your fish, darling. It's brain food." Or worse, "Eat your liver, it keeps the blood red." But the most detested directives were those involving vegetables. "Broccoli is good roughage." Or, "Try just ONE Brussels sprout, it will protect you from, from . . . everything bad!" Then there were carrots, which I didn't mind too much in their raw state, but cooked? Feh! "Eat them! They're good for your eyes."

Of course, mother was right. In fact, carrots are indeed good for our eyesight because they're rich in beta carotene which the body converts to Vitamin A, a crucial nutrient for the functioning of the retina. I'm glad most of mother's cajoling worked, because I have grown to welcome and enjoy most of the items on her "most needed" list of foods.

This delicious recipe is a clever way to get to know and love carrot soup. Enhanced by sherry and a hint of apple juice, it is a wonderful beginning for your most elegant dinner.

2   cups carrots, scraped and shredded
3   cups low sodium chicken broth
1   tablespoon thawed frozen apple juice concentrate
1   small onion, finely chopped
    Water

2   tablespoons sherry
½   teaspoon nutmeg, preferably freshly grated
     Salt and freshly ground pepper to taste
4   teaspoons chopped fresh chives

1. Combine carrots, broth, apple juice concentrate, and onion in a large saucepan. Bring to a boil, cover, lower heat, and simmer gently for 20 minutes or until carrots are very tender.

2. Transfer contents of saucepan to a food processor and puree (do this in several batches if necessary).

3. Return puree to the saucepan and stir over very low heat for 2 minutes or until heated through, adding water, a ¼ cup at a time, if mixture is very thick. Swirl in sherry and nutmeg, taste and add salt and pepper, and serve sprinkled with chives.

SERVES 4
APPROXIMATELY 77 CALORIES PER SERVING

RED CABBAGE SOUP WITH TURKEY SAUSAGE

▶ ▶

This recipe pays homage to old-fashioned Russian cabbage soup but uses the lovely red cabbage instead of green, lower fat turkey sausage instead of flanken, and wine. It is a sumptuous, zesty soup that will finish in under two hours.

All you'll need for a complete and comforting meal is a dollop of light sour cream (15 calories per tablespoon) or nonfat plain yogurt (7 calories per tablespoon) and a loaf of aromatic Russian black bread.

    1   teaspoon olive oil
    4   ounces turkey sausage, preferably kielbasa,
        casings removed
    1   large onion, thinly sliced and cut in half
    2   large cloves garlic, minced
  1/2   cup dry red wine
    1   small head red cabbage (about 1 1/4 pounds),
        cored and shredded
    1   cup low sodium tomato sauce
    3   cups low sodium chicken broth
  1/2   teaspoon dried sage
    1   tablespoon minced fresh parsley or 2 teaspoons
        dried
        Salt and freshly ground pepper to taste

1. Heat oil in a large stockpot or kettle. Add turkey and stir over medium-high heat, breaking up chunks with a

---

wooden spoon, until lightly browned. Reduce heat to medium, add onion and garlic, and cook, stirring often, for 5 minutes.

2. Add wine and cabbage and bring to a boil. Reduce heat, cover, and cook over very low heat, stirring occasionally, for 10 minutes or until cabbage is soft.

3. Add remaining ingredients, stir well, cover, and cook over very low heat for 1½ hours, stirring occasionally, and adding a little water if soup seems dry.

SERVES 4
APPROXIMATELY 156 CALORIES PER SERVING

♦ ♦ ♦ ♦ ♦

HOT MULLIGATAWNY SOUP

▶ ▶

To the people who inhabit southern India, *mulligatawny* translates to "pepper water." It is a soup that is based on a rich meat (although never beef) or vegetable broth which is highly spiced with curry and other seasonings. Bits of chicken are often contained in this magnificently complex concoction. But natives may also include rice, eggs, coconut shreds, and sometimes cream.

This mulligatawny is excellent as a one-dish meal along with a simple salad and warmed Indian-style or pita bread.

3¹/₂	cups low sodium chicken broth
1	medium onion, chopped
1¹/₂	tablespoons all-purpose flour
1	tablespoon curry powder
¹/₄	teaspoon nutmeg
¹/₈	teaspoon cayenne pepper (*optional if using hot curry powder*)
2	cups peeled, chopped tomatoes, fresh or no-salt-added canned, undrained
1	large carrot, diced
1	large rib celery, diced
1	bay leaf
³/₄	cup cooked rice
1¹/₂	cups cooked, diced white meat chicken
	Salt and freshly ground pepper to taste
³/₄	cup low fat (1%) milk

4   tablespoons nonfat plain yogurt
4   tablespoons chopped fresh parsley

1. Heat 2 tablespoons broth in a large stockpot or kettle. Braise onion over medium-low heat until translucent, adding additional broth, if necessary, to keep onion from burning.

2. Stir in flour, curry powder, nutmeg, and cayenne if desired, and cook, stirring, for 1 minute or until flour is dissolved. Add 1/2 cup broth and stir until blended.

3. Raise heat to medium, add remaining broth, tomatoes and juice, carrot, celery, bay leaf, and rice. Cook over medium heat for 10 minutes or until slightly thickened. Reduce heat, cover, and simmer for 20 minutes or until carrots and celery are tender.

4. Add chicken and heat through. Taste and add salt and pepper, if desired. Stir in milk and heat through, but do not boil. Serve in individual bowls, each garnished with 1 tablespoon yogurt blended with 1 tablespoon chopped parsley.

SERVES 4

APPROXIMATELY 261 CALORIES PER SERVING

SUMMER SQUASH SOUP
WITH FRESH CHILIES

▶▶▶▶▶▶▶▶▶▶▶▶▶▶▶▶▶▶▶▶▶▶▶▶▶▶▶

The vegetables make this soup nutritional; the chilies make it exciting. I make this soup frequently, rotating the supporting cast of vegetables around the zucchini and yellow squash according to freshness and availability at the market. Handle chilies carefully; they can burn.

1	tablespoon canola oil
5	serrano chilies, stems and seeds removed, sliced into rings (wear rubber gloves)
1	small onion, chopped
2	stalks celery, chopped
2	medium zucchini, thinly sliced
1	medium yellow squash, thinly sliced
½	cup small, young green peas, fresh or frozen and thawed
½	cup sliced fresh green beans
4	cups low sodium chicken broth
2	ripe small round or plum tomatoes, peeled and chopped
	Salt and freshly ground pepper to taste
¼	cup chopped fresh cilantro
4	teaspoons light sour cream

1. In a large, nonstick skillet, heat the oil and sauté the chilies, onion, and celery over medium heat for about 5 minutes or until softened.

2. Add the zucchini, yellow squash, peas, beans, and broth. Bring to a boil, reduce heat and simmer for about 15 minutes or until squash is nearly tender.

3. Stir in the tomatoes and simmer for an additional 15 minutes. Taste and add salt, if desired, pepper, and cilantro. Garnish each serving with a teaspoon of sour cream.

SERVES 4
APPROXIMATELY 170 CALORIES PER SERVING

SALMON AND VEGETABLE CHOWDER

▶ ▶

$\mathbb{H}$ere is a soup of such rich and velvety elegance you won't believe how easy it is to prepare. Serve with a salad alongside and berries for dessert and you have a complete low-cal meal.

³/₄	pound fresh salmon fillet, or 13-ounce can red salmon, drained, skinned, boned, and coarsely flaked
2¹/₂	cups water
1	cup low sodium chicken broth
1	medium carrot, diced
1	small clove garlic, minced
1	medium onion, chopped
1	medium stalk celery, diced
2	medium potatoes, peeled and cubed
1	teaspoon dried parsley
¹/₂	teaspoon dried thyme
¹/₂	cup tiny green peas, fresh or frozen and thawed
1	cup evaporated low fat milk
	Salt and freshly ground pepper to taste

1. If using fresh salmon, place fillet in a large stockpot or kettle with 1¹/₂ cups water, and bring to a simmer over medium heat. Cover, reduce heat, and simmer gently for 5 minutes or until salmon loses its transparency. Remove salmon, reserving liquid in pot, and set salmon aside. If using canned salmon, proceed to the next step.

2. Add water (remaining 1 cup if using fresh salmon) to pot, along with the rest of the ingredients, except salmon, peas, milk, and salt and pepper. Bring to a boil, cover, reduce heat, and simmer gently for 10 minutes or until vegetables are tender.

3. Add peas and salmon (if using fresh salmon, remove and discard skin and flake coarsely). Simmer over medium-low heat, stirring occasionally, for 5 minutes. Stir in milk and heat through but do not boil. Taste and correct seasonings.

SERVES 4

APPROXIMATELY 285 CALORIES PER SERVING

◆ ◆ ◆ ◆

HOT AND SOUR
FISH CHOWDER

▶ ▶

I first enjoyed this soup at a New York Chinatown eatery where much more attention was paid to the cuisine than to the ambience. Here the menu, which had roughly the same amount of text as *War and Peace,* was scripted in Chinese—without benefit of translation. The waiters, although earnest and hardworking, were largely unfamiliar with the English language and we were usually reduced to ordering by pointing to attractive-looking and fragrant-smelling dishes we saw the Chinese patrons eating. For the most part, this method worked.

It was at this nameless restaurant known only by its numbered address that I first saw a party of four locals happily going at a soup with the most wonderful aroma and color. I simply had to order it for myself. I was not to be disappointed, for out came a hot and sour soup very similar to the one I've described below.

This dish makes a very satisfying lunch or first course of a dinner that might include poached chicken breast slices with crunchy bean sprouts and just-steamed broccoli or string beans drizzled with a light soy dressing.

¹/₂	pound cod fillets, diced
¹/₂	tablespoon dry sherry
¹/₂	tablespoon freshly minced ginger root
2¹/₂	tablespoons cornstarch
2	teaspoons canola or other light oil

1   medium leek, white and tender greens, well
    rinsed and coarsely chopped
3   cups low sodium chicken broth
¼   cup canned, drained, and shredded bamboo
    shoots
4   dried Shiitake mushrooms, stemmed, soaked 30
    minutes in hot water, then drained and chopped
½   cup drained and diced firm tofu
2   teaspoons low sodium soy sauce
2   tablespoons white vinegar
¼   teaspoon white pepper, or to taste
3   tablespoons water
    Dash hot pepper sauce, or to taste
2   scallions, white and tender greens, minced

1. Combine cod, sherry, ginger, and ½ tablespoon cornstarch in a bowl and set aside.

2. Heat oil in a nonstick saucepan over medium-low
heat and sauté leek, stirring often, for about 5 minutes or
until softened.

3. Raise heat, add broth, and bring to a boil. Add fish
mixture and stir gently to separate the pieces. Add bamboo
shoots and chopped mushrooms. Return to a boil and cook
for 2 minutes. Drop in tofu, add soy sauce, and return to a boil
once more.

4. Stir in vinegar, pepper, remaining 2 tablespoons
cornstarch dissolved in 3 tablespoons water, and hot pepper
sauce. Cook over low heat, stirring constantly, until soup has
thickened. Pour into individual heated bowls and serve garnished with scallions.

SERVES 4 GENEROUSLY
APPROXIMATELY 205 CALORIES PER SERVING

LIGHT CLAM CHOWDER, NEW ENGLAND STYLE

▶ ▶

*O*nce you assemble the necessary ingredients and have everything ready for cooking, I promise this sensational chowder will be a breeze to complete and a joy to eat. The dish can also be prepared a day ahead, refrigerated, and re-heated (without boiling), then garnished prior to serving.

2	*dozen littleneck clams, scrubbed*
1	*cup cold water*
	Vegetable oil cooking spray
1	*teaspoon canola or other light oil*
2	*medium onions (or 1 onion and 1 leek), chopped*
2	*medium celery stalks with leaves, trimmed and chopped*
1	*large carrot, cut in half lengthwise and thinly sliced*
2	*tablespoons extra lean (95% fat free) boiled ham, minced*
2	*medium cloves garlic, minced*
5	*fresh parsley sprigs*
1	*fresh thyme sprig or ¹/₂ teaspoon dried thyme*
1	*pound boiling potatoes, peeled and cubed*
16	*ounces bottled clam juice, approximately*
1	*cup evaporated low fat milk*
	Salt and freshly ground pepper to taste
	Dash hot pepper sauce, or to taste
2	*tablespoons chopped fresh parsley*
	Paprika

1. Combine clams and water in a large pot. Bring water to a boil, cover, and steam clams for 5 minutes or just until they open. Transfer clams to a bowl, discarding any that have not opened. Strain steaming liquid and reserve.

2. Heat cooking spray and oil in the same pot. Add onions, celery, carrot, ham, garlic, parsley, and thyme. Cover and cook over low heat, stirring occasionally, for 8 minutes or until vegetables are tender.

3. Add potatoes, reserved steaming liquid, and enough clam juice to cover vegetables. Cover and simmer gently for 15 minutes or until potatoes are tender.

4. Discard thyme sprig, if used. Transfer half of the vegetables and ½ cup cooking liquid to a food processor and puree. Return pureed vegetables to pot (if you prefer a thicker chowder, puree more vegetables; for a thinner chowder, add additional clam juice at 6 calories a half cup).

5. Add milk and heat to just below simmering—do not boil.

6. Remove clams from shells and add to chowder. Season with salt and pepper and hot sauce, if desired. Ladle into warmed soup bowls and garnish with parsley and paprika.

SERVES 4
APPROXIMATELY 235 CALORIES PER SERVING

♦ ♦ ♦ ♦ ♦

CHILLED BEET AND CUCUMBER SOUP

▶ ▶

Quick and simple to put together, the subtle flavors of this cool, refreshing soup are further enhanced with dill. Serve in frosted glass goblets garnished with wisps of fresh dill for an extra touch of luxury.

    1   cup low fat buttermilk
    2   cups low fat plain yogurt
    ¼   cup apple juice
    1   large beet, cooked, peeled, and diced, or 1 cup
        canned and drained diced beets
    2   medium cucumbers, peeled, seeded, and diced
    6   scallions, white part only, thinly sliced
    2   tablespoons minced fresh dill weed or 2 teaspoons
        dried
        Salt and freshly ground pepper to taste

Combine buttermilk, yogurt, and apple juice in a large mixing bowl. Stir until well blended. Stir in remaining ingredients. Cover and refrigerate for 2 hours before serving.

SERVES 4
APPROXIMATELY 157 CALORIES PER SERVING

MEATS

♦ ♦ ♦ ♦ ♦

BELGIAN BEEF AND ONION STEW

▶ ▶

In this recipe, the beef cubes are first broiled to dispose of most of the superfluous fat while producing a browned crust to intensify the taste. After the onions are sautéed, a bit of broth is added to help them caramelize. Once the beef and onions are combined with the vegetables, herbs, and spices, the stew is simmered in a heady brew of beer and broth to fully integrate the flavors.

1	pound beef top round, trimmed of all visible fat and cubed
	Vegetable oil cooking spray
1	teaspoon olive oil
2	large onions, thinly sliced or chopped
1/4	cup low sodium beef broth or bouillon
2	large carrots, cut into pieces
12	fluid ounces beer, regular or nonalcoholic
	Pinch allspice
	Salt and freshly ground pepper to taste
1/2	teaspoon dried thyme
1/2	teaspoon dried savory
1	large bay leaf
1	teaspoon sugar (optional)

1. Preheat broiler.

2. Arrange beef cubes on rack set on a baking sheet and broil close to heat source, turning occasionally, until meat is browned. Remove from oven and set aside on paper towels to drain.

3. Coat a large saucepan or kettle with cooking spray and oil and sauté onions over medium-low heat, stirring occasionally, until well wilted. Raise heat to medium, add broth and cook until broth has evaporated and onions are browned.

4. Add beef, carrots, beer, allspice, salt to taste, several grindings of pepper, thyme, savory, bay leaf, and enough water to cover meat. Bring mixture to a boil, cover, reduce heat to very low, and cook for 2 hours or until beef is fork tender. Check and add additional water if liquid evaporates below the level of the meat. Taste and add sugar if mixture is at all bitter.

5. Cool stew, then refrigerate. When well chilled, remove any fat that has accumulated on the surface. Reheat gently before serving.

SERVES 4
APPROXIMATELY 185 CALORIES PER SERVING
APPROXIMATELY 189 CALORIES PER SERVING WITH SUGAR

♦ ♦ ♦ ♦ ♦

BEEF AND BEAN CHILI BURRITOS

▶ ▶

Unlike chili con carne, which is predominately a meat dish, this chili makes equal partners of beef and beans.

Burritos are traditionally served with salsa and bowls of chopped tomatoes, onions, and light (for our dietary purposes) sour cream (15 calories per tablespoon). This dish is fun to prepare and eat.

³/₄	*pound extra lean ground beef*
1	*small onion, diced*
¹/₂	*green bell pepper, diced*
1	*clove garlic, minced*
¹/₂	*teaspoon pure ground red chili pepper, or to taste*
¹/₄	*teaspoon ground cumin*
	Pinch dried oregano
¹/₄	*cup dry red wine*
1	*cup low sodium tomato sauce*
¹/₂	*cup cooked pinto beans*
¹/₂	*teaspoon salt, or to taste*
4	*flour tortillas, 9-inch diameter*
2	*scallions, white and tender greens, chopped*
1	*cup Jalapeño Salsa (page 7) or bottled burrito sauce*
2	*tablespoons shredded Monterey jack cheese*
3	*cups coarsely shredded romaine lettuce*

1. Heat a large nonstick skillet over medium heat, add beef and cook, stirring and breaking up large pieces with a

wooden spoon, until meat loses its pink color. Tip skillet and pour off all accumulated fat.

2. Add onions to skillet and cook over medium heat for 5 minutes or until meat is well browned and onion is wilted.

3. Add bell pepper, garlic, ground chili, cumin, and oregano. Cook, stirring, for 2 minutes, then pour in wine and tomato sauce. Reduce heat and cook for 15 minutes at a bare simmer to blend flavors, then add beans and heat through. Mixture should be thick. Taste and add salt, if desired.

4. While chili simmers, preheat oven to 300°F.

5. Place one tortilla on each of four ovenproof serving dishes and set in oven for 5 minutes or until tortillas are well heated but not crispy. Remove from oven, but do not turn off heat.

6. Spoon about ½ cup of beef-chili mixture down the center of each tortilla. Cover beef with a sprinkling of chopped scallion and fold tortilla over filling. Top with Jalapeño Salsa or burrito sauce and sprinkle shredded cheese over sauce. Place burritos in oven just long enough for cheese to soften. Remove from oven, surround burritos with shredded lettuce, and serve.

SERVES 4

APPROXIMATELY 359 CALORIES PER SERVING

MINI MEAT LOAVES

▶ ▶

Designed so that everyone gets their own end-pieces of the meatloaf, these mini loaves can be served with fresh corn on the cob and a salad. Chilled and sliced, they are also terrific for sandwiches, picnics, and brown-bagging it to work. Reusable mini-loaf pans are available in most supermarkets, but free-form loaves are fine.

1¹/₄	pounds lean ground beef
1	cup cooked brown rice
1	medium onion, finely chopped
2	large egg whites
¹/₂	cup peeled, coarsely chopped tomatoes, fresh or canned
¹/₄	cup chopped fresh parsley
1¹/₂	teaspoons ground cumin
1	tablespoon tomato paste
	Salt and freshly ground pepper to taste

1. Preheat oven to 350°F.

2. Combine all ingredients, mixing lightly with a wooden spoon or your hands. Do not overwork the meat.

3. Divide mixture into six mini loaves and bake for 40 minutes (cover loaves with foil for the last 10 minutes if they are already well browned).

SERVES 6

APPROXIMATELY 311 CALORIES PER SERVING

◆ ◆ ◆ ◆ ◆

VEAL MEDALLIONS
WITH SOUSED MUSHROOMS

▶ ▶

This dish has precisely the qualities I look for in a main course: it is quick to prepare and has superior flavor. Here, cultivated and exotic mushrooms get the opportunity to party with Cognac, shallots, garlic, and herbs until they all achieve an agreeable buzz.

The preparation is so easy that more attention may be paid to accompanying dishes. Greens and Beans (page 172), Green and Yellow Beans Balsamic (page 176), or any roasted or grilled vegetable may be presented to great advantage.

$1/4$ ounce dried porcini mushrooms
$1/3$ cup very warm water
$1^1/2$ cups low sodium beef broth
2   teaspoons olive oil
    Olive oil cooking spray
1   small shallot, chopped
1   small clove garlic, finely minced
5   ounces fresh mushrooms, wiped clean, trimmed, and thinly sliced
1   tablespoon Cognac or other unflavored brandy
$1/2$ tablespoon chopped fresh thyme or $1/2$ teaspoon dried
$1/2$ tablespoon chopped fresh rosemary or $1/2$ teaspoon dried
4   veal tenderloin medallions (about 4 ounces each), flattened to about $1/2$ inch thick

1 tablespoon superfine flour
Juice of 1 large lemon
Salt and freshly ground pepper to taste

1. Soak porcini mushrooms in warm water for 45 minutes.

2. Meanwhile, boil beef broth in a small saucepan until reduced to about ¾ cup. Set aside and keep warm.

3. Heat 1 teaspoon of the olive oil in a nonstick saucepan coated with cooking spray. Add shallot and garlic and sauté over medium heat, shaking pan frequently, for 2 minutes.

4. Add fresh mushrooms and cook for 5 minutes or until mushroom liquid is nearly evaporated. Remove pan from heat, pour in Cognac, and light carefully. Shake pan until flames are extinguished (this should happen quickly).

5. Drain and slice porcini mushrooms and reserve liquid. Add reserved liquid to skillet, along with reduced broth. Raise heat to medium-high and cook until liquid is reduced by about half. Add sliced porcinis, thyme, and rosemary and cook, stirring, for 4 minutes. Remove from heat, cover and keep warm.

6. Spray a large nonstick skillet with cooking oil and add remaining teaspoon olive oil. Dredge veal lightly in flour, shaking off any excess, and sauté quickly over medium-high heat for 1 or 2 minutes per side or until just cooked.

7. Reduce heat, squeeze lemon juice over the veal medallions and sprinkle lightly with salt and freshly ground pepper. Pour sauce into skillet and shake to coat the veal.

SERVES 4
APPROXIMATELY 180 CALORIES PER SERVING

COLD VEAL ROAST
WITH TUNA SAUCE

▶ ▶

M y adaptation of *vitello tonnato* eliminates oil completely and substitutes low fat yogurt for the mayonnaise. The result is a substantial savings in calories and fat without sacrificing the subtle flavor and delicious taste.

For a wonderful warm weather lunch or light dinner, try it with rice (cooled to room temperature), and a side dish of fresh ripe tomato and cucumber slices.

2³/₄	pounds lean, boneless veal roast, preferably cut from the leg, rolled and tied
1	6¹/₈-ounce can water-packed white tuna (*low sodium if desired*)
2	medium onions, chopped
2	stalks celery, chopped
1	carrot, chopped
2	garlic cloves, cut in half
4	anchovies, rinsed, drained, and chopped
1	tablespoon minced fresh parsley
1	teaspoon dried thyme
	Salt and freshly ground pepper to taste
1¹/₂	cups water
1	cup low sodium chicken broth
¹/₄	cup dry white wine
³/₄	cup low fat plain yogurt
2	tablespoons fresh lemon juice
2	tablespoons capers, rinsed and drained
	Lemon wedges and parsley sprigs for garnish

1. Place veal in a heavy stockpot with a tight-fitting cover. Add all remaining ingredients, except yogurt, lemon juice, capers, and garnish, and bring to a boil. Reduce heat, cover, and simmer over very low heat for 1½ hours or until veal is tender, turning meat once during cooking.

2. Raise heat to medium and cook, uncovered, until liquid is reduced by half. Remove from heat and cool to room temperature, then cover and refrigerate pot with its ingredients for 8 hours or overnight.

3. Remove from refrigerator and skim off any fat that has accumulated on surface of veal and sauce. Remove veal from pot and transfer to a cutting board.

4. Transfer remaining contents of pot to a food processor and process until coarsely pureed. Add yogurt and lemon juice and process for 5 seconds. Transfer sauce to a mixing bowl and stir in capers.

5. Cut veal into very thin slices. Arrange slices on a serving platter, overlapping them slightly. Using about ½ cup of the sauce, pour a wide ribbon down the center of the veal slices. Garnish platter with lemon wedges and parsley sprigs and serve accompanied with remaining sauce on the side.

SERVES 8

APPROXIMATELY 234 CALORIES PER SERVING

VEAL BRAISED
WITH MUSHROOMS AND WINE

▶ ▶

This dish is delicious with cooked rice and peas.

	Vegetable oil cooking spray
1	pound veal shoulder, trimmed of all visible fat and cut into 1-inch cubes
1	large shallot, minced
1	small onion, thinly sliced
1	cup medium-dry white wine
1/2	pound small fresh mushrooms, wiped clean and trimmed
1	small stalk celery, thinly sliced
1	small carrot, thinly sliced
1	large clove garlic, minced
1/2	teaspoon dried thyme
1/2	cup low sodium chicken broth, approximately

1. Coat a large skillet with cooking spray and heat. Add veal and cook over medium-high heat, turning to brown on all sides and removing cubes to a bowl as they brown. When all the veal has been browned, pour off any accumulated fat from the skillet but do not wipe it clean.

2. Add shallot and onion to skillet, reduce heat to medium, and cook, stirring often, until onion is translucent.

3. Pour in wine and cook, stirring and scraping any browned bits from the bottom of skillet, for 1 minute.

4. Reduce heat to medium-low, return veal to skillet along with mushrooms, celery, carrot, garlic, and thyme. Add

enough broth to just cover meat. (If additional broth is needed, add 9 calories per ¼ cup.) Cover and simmer very gently for 1 hour, stirring occasionally and adding small amounts of broth, if necessary, to keep meat covered.

SERVES 4 GENEROUSLY
APPROXIMATELY 165 CALORIES PER SERVING

◆ ◆ ◆ ◆ ◆

GRILLED BUTTERFLIED
LEG OF LAMB

▶ ▶

Marinating is a terrific way to remove the gamey quality from lamb that some people find unpleasant, so don't be tempted to cut the marinating time short.

When cooked, transfer the lamb to a cutting board and let it rest so that the natural juices redistribute evenly throughout the meat. Then slice and serve with the delicious juices and perhaps crisp-steamed cauliflower and broccoli florets flavored with lemon juice.

5¹/₂	pounds bone-in leg of lamb
1	tablespoon Dijon mustard
2	large cloves garlic, minced
¹/₄	cup fresh lemon juice
1	teaspoon dried crumbled mint
¹/₂	teaspoon dried rosemary
¹/₂	teaspoon dried thyme
¹/₄	cup chopped fresh parsley
³/₄	cup low fat plain yogurt
	Salt and freshly ground pepper to taste

1. Have the lamb boned, trimmed of all visible fat, and butterflied. (You should end up with about 3¹/₂ pounds of raw lamb.)

2. In a dish large enough to accommodate the lamb, combine all remaining ingredients. Pierce the lamb with a fork in several places and spread with marinade, turning the

lamb to cover all sides. Cover and refrigerate the lamb for at least 8 hours. (You can prepare the marinade the night before, cover the lamb in the morning, and the meat will be ready to grill that evening.)

3. Prepare grill or preheat broiler.

4. Remove lamb from the marinade and grill or broil for about 15 minutes per side for medium. Salt lightly just before serving, if desired.

SERVES **8**
APPROXIMATELY **273** CALORIES PER SERVING

SPICY LAMB KEBABS

▶ ▶

Because the flavor of this dish is so powerful, serve just a simple rice or mildly flavored lentil dish as an accompaniment.

1	pound lean boneless lamb, trimmed of all visible fat and cut into 1-inch cubes
1	small yellow onion, grated or pureed in food processor
1	tablespoon freshly grated ginger root
2	large cloves garlic, minced
	Juice of 3 large lemons
1	tablespoon tomato paste
1	tablespoon peanut oil
$1/2$	teaspoon each: ground coriander, cumin, and turmeric
$1/8$	teaspoon ground nutmeg or four grindings fresh nutmeg
$1/8$	teaspoon ground cinnamon
$1/4$	teaspoon hot paprika, or to taste
2	tablespoons finely chopped fresh cilantro or parsley

1. Combine all ingredients in a baking dish or bowl and refrigerate lamb for at least 4 hours (the longer the better), turning lamb often.

2. Prepare grill or preheat broiler.

3. Thread kebabs on skewers (if you are using bamboo

sticks, soak them in water first), allowing a small space between chunks of lamb for even cooking, and grill or broil, turning often, for about 12 minutes for medium.

SERVES 4
APPROXIMATELY 206 CALORIES PER SERVING

◆ ◆ ◆ ◆ ◆

SWEET AND SAVORY STUFFED PORK

▶ ▶

This recipe is specifically for pork tenderloin which is one of the leanest cuts of meat available. As with other meats, when portions are moderate and all visible fat is trimmed, pork (at least the tenderloin) can be a perfectly acceptable component of a well-balanced diet. Serve with oven-roasted potato wedges and Carrot Puree (page 180).

Vegetable oil cooking spray
1 pound pork tenderloin, trimmed of all visible fat
1 cup whole wheat bread crumbs
1/4 cup dry sherry
2 tablespoons low sodium chicken broth
1 teaspoon dried rosemary, crumbled
1 teaspoon dried thyme, crumbled
1 tablespoon apricot fruit spread (no sugar added)
3 cloves garlic, pressed
1 tablespoon coarse-grained mustard

1. Preheat oven to 375°F. Coat a shallow roasting pan lightly with cooking spray and set aside.

2. Cut tenderloin down the center lengthwise to within 1/2 inch of the bottom. Spread open, place between sheets of wax paper, and pound to an even thickness of about 1/4 inch.

3. Combine bread crumbs, sherry, broth, rosemary, and thyme. Toss with a fork until completely moistened.

4. Combine fruit spread with garlic and mustard. Spread evenly over exposed side of roast and cover with bread crumb

mixture. Roll roast and tie at 2-inch intervals with kitchen string.

5. Put rolled roast in center of prepared roasting pan, seam side down. Roast for 50 minutes.

6. Remove from oven and let stand, loosely tented with foil, for 5 minutes. Cut away string, cut roast into thin slices, and arrange on a heated serving platter.

SERVES 4

APPROXIMATELY 221 CALORIES PER SERVING

POULTRY

◆ ◆ ◆ ◆ ◆

STEWED CHICKEN WITH ARTICHOKES AND WATERCRESS

▶▶▶▶▶▶▶▶▶▶▶▶▶▶▶▶▶▶▶▶▶▶▶▶▶

This unusual but felicitous combination is one I have enjoyed often through the years. Rice, barley, bulgur, or any other plain cooked grain would be perfect served alongside to soak up the sauce.

2½	pounds chicken, skinned, trimmed of all visible fat and cut into 8 serving pieces
3	cups water
1	cup low sodium chicken broth
¾	cup dry vermouth or white wine
2	stalks celery, with tops, chopped
1	large onion, diced
4 to 6	parsley sprigs
½	teaspoon dried tarragon
6 to 8	whole peppercorns
	Salt to taste
2	large cloves garlic, pressed
1	tablespoon fresh lemon juice
¼	cup chopped fresh parsley
1½	cups chopped fresh watercress
2	teaspoons cornstarch dissolved in ¼ cup cool water
1½	cups artichoke hearts, water-packed, drained, or frozen and thawed

1. In a large pot, combine chicken with water, broth, wine, celery, onion, parsley, tarragon, peppercorns, and salt

if desired. Bring to a boil, cover, reduce heat, and simmer gently for 45 minutes or until chicken is just tender.

2. Remove chicken from pot and set aside. Strain cooking liquid, discarding solids. Measure out 2½ cups of liquid (if necessary, add water).

3. Return 2½ cups strained liquid to pot. Add garlic, lemon juice, parsley, and watercress, and cook over medium heat for 5 minutes, stirring often.

4. Add dissolved cornstarch and water to pot and stir over medium heat until mixture just starts to thicken. Reduce heat, add chicken pieces and artichoke hearts, cover, and simmer very gently for an additional 10 minutes.

SERVES 4

APPROXIMATELY 213 CALORIES PER SERVING

◆ ◆ ◆ ◆ ◆

GRILLED CHICKEN
WITH PEAR CHUTNEY

▶ ▶

Chutney is a condiment containing fruit, vinegar, sugar, and spices. The texture can range from chunky to smooth and it may either be mild, hot, Hot, or HOT! Although there are good commercial brands available in markets today, I find that they are often too sweet. Chutney is quite easy to make as you'll discover when you try the pear variety described below.

The natural partner to curried dishes and baked or grilled poultry, chutney is also terrific spread on bread or spooned over low fat cottage cheese. Serve this great chicken-chutney combo with herbed wild rice and cucumber salad.

1/4	cup fresh lime juice
1	clove garlic, minced
1	teaspoon mild mustard
2	whole boneless, skinless chicken breasts (about 1 1/4 pounds), halved and trimmed of all visible fat

PEAR CHUTNEY

2	ripe pears, preferably Bartlett, peeled, cored, and cubed
1	tart apple, preferably Granny Smith, peeled, cored, and cubed
1/2	medium red onion, coarsely chopped
1	large clove garlic, pressed

$^1/_2$ cup cider vinegar
   Juice of 1 large lemon
 2 teaspoons sugar
$^1/_2$ teaspoon each: ground coriander, cumin,
   nutmeg, and ginger

1. In a large, shallow bowl or baking dish, combine lime juice with garlic and mustard. Place chicken breasts in marinade and turn to coat. Cover dish and refrigerate for 1 hour.

2. Prepare chutney by combining all remaining ingredients in a large saucepan. Bring to a boil, stirring often, then reduce heat and simmer gently, uncovered, for 30 minutes or until fruit is soft.

3. Prepare grill or preheat broiler.

4. Grill or broil chicken breasts for about 8 to 10 minutes per side depending on thickness of pieces, basting occasionally with marinade.

5. Transfer chicken to 4 plates and serve with equal portions of warmed chutney.

SERVES 4
APPROXIMATELY 251 CALORIES PER SERVING
APPROXIMATELY 159 CALORIES PER SERVING WITHOUT CHUTNEY

♦ ♦ ♦ ♦ ♦

CHICKEN CACCIATORE

▶ ▶

The byword these days is *retro*, the term used to describe resurrected trends in everything from food to fashion to furnishings. Retro may refer to something that was considered homey, homely, or even tacky in its prime but, in the minds of today's awareness-gurus, is now considered too good to be neglected, eradicated, or ignored.

Chicken Cacciatore is one of those back-to-the-future items. Way back when, this lusty dish was featured on just about any well-rounded Italian menu. Of course, the good old days were also the bad fat, high calorie days.

Today, cacciatore has seen the light. With a more cautious hand and an educated head, we've rediscovered this classic hunter-style creation.

2	teaspoons olive oil
1¹/₄	pounds boneless, skinless chicken breasts, trimmed of all visible fat and cut into chunks
2	medium onions, chopped
1	large clove garlic, minced
3	ounces fresh small mushrooms, wiped clean, stems trimmed
1	teaspoon dried crumbled oregano or marjoram
3	tablespoons balsamic or red wine vinegar
5	tablespoons no-salt-added tomato paste
2	cups low sodium chicken broth
1	cup dry red wine
2	chopped fresh basil leaves or ¹/₂ teaspoon dried

Salt and freshly ground pepper to taste
2   *tablespoons chopped fresh parsley*

1. Heat oil in a large nonstick skillet. Add chicken and brown on all sides. Remove chicken to a bowl and set aside.

2. Add onion and garlic to skillet and cook over medium heat for about 3 minutes or until onion is just translucent.

3. Add mushrooms, oregano, vinegar, and tomato paste. Raise heat and cook, stirring, until thoroughly blended. Return chicken to skillet, along with any accumulated juices in bowl.

4. Stir in broth, wine, and basil and bring to a boil. Reduce heat, cover, and simmer gently for 10 to 15 minutes or until chicken is thoroughly cooked. Taste and add salt and pepper, if desired. Serve sprinkled with parsley.

SERVES 4
APPROXIMATELY 229 CALORIES PER SERVING

◆ ◆ ◆ ◆

"BUFFALO" CHICKEN BREASTS

▶ ▶

Lately one of my most requested recipes is this stream-lined version of Buffalo wings—those spicy, deep-fried chicken wings served with bowls of chunky blue cheese dressing for dipping and popularized by the winter-worn denizens of Buffalo, New York.

This recipe eliminates the deep frying and even the wings themselves, but retains the zesty taste of that spicy chicken dish. You can moderate the heat by adding or reducing the amount of hot sauce in the marinade.

   1/4   *cup nonfat plain yogurt*
   1/4   *teaspoon lemon juice*
    2   *teaspoons hot pepper sauce, or to taste*
    2   *whole boneless, skinless chicken breasts (about 1
         pound), halved and trimmed of all visible fat*
   1/4   *cup fine dry bread crumbs*
         Vegetable oil cooking spray
         Salt to taste

   1. In a shallow dish, combine yogurt, lemon juice, and hot sauce. Add chicken and turn to coat all sides. Cover and refrigerate for 2 hours, occasionally turning chicken in mari-nade.
   2. Preheat oven to 350°F.
   3. Remove chicken from marinade and dredge in bread crumbs, pressing lightly to help crumbs adhere. Refrigerate for 15 minutes.
   4. Arrange chicken breasts in one layer in a baking dish

coated lightly with cooking spray. Bake for 35 minutes or until chicken is cooked through. Sprinkle lightly with salt, if desired.

SERVES 4
APPROXIMATELY 154 CALORIES PER SERVING

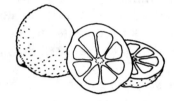

CHICKEN CRUSTED
WITH HERBS AND MUSTARD

▶▶▶▶▶▶▶▶▶▶▶▶▶▶▶▶▶▶▶▶▶▶▶▶▶▶

Chicken is blessed with a unique, delicate, almost neutral flavor that makes it hospitable to many other ingredients. One of the more versatile meats, it marries well with herbs as assertive as rosemary and sage, and with bold spices including mustard, especially when honey is used as a buffer. That is the combination used in the recipe below.

The bulk of the preparation time is devoted to the marination; the total cooking time is a hasty half hour.

> 1   tablespoon Dijon mustard
> 1   tablespoon coarse-grained or country-style
>   mustard
> 1   tablespoon honey
> 1/2 teaspoon each: dried rosemary, sage, and thyme
>   (or your favorite herb blend)
> 1/4 cup dry white wine
> 1   medium clove garlic, minced
> 2   whole chicken breasts with bone (about 2
>   pounds), skinned, halved, and trimmed of all
>   visible fat
> 1/3 cup fine dry bread crumbs
>   Lemon or lime wedges for garnish

1. In a small bowl, combine mustards, honey, and herbs, whisking or stirring well to combine. Set 1 tablespoon

of the mixture aside and combine the rest with the wine and garlic.

2. In a shallow dish large enough to hold the chicken pieces in one layer, refrigerate the chicken in the wine and mustard mixture, turning occasionally, for at least 2 hours.

3. Preheat oven to 350°F.

4. Combine the reserved tablespoon of mustard mixture with the bread crumbs. Pat mixture onto the meaty part of the breasts, pressing lightly so the mixture adheres, and arrange breasts on a baking sheet. Bake for 30 minutes or until chicken is just tender. Set oven to broil and brown chicken for 5 minutes or until cooked through and golden. Serve immediately with fresh lemon or lime wedges.

SERVES 4

APPROXIMATELY 221 CALORIES PER SERVING

◆ ◆ ◆ ◆ ◆

CHICKEN AND ASPARAGUS, JAPANESE STYLE

▶ ▶

For those who have wondered if there is life after sushi— the answer is a resounding Yes! Try this Japanese-style chicken.

Slightly crusty on the outside and juicy-moist within, these breasts of chicken are marinated in a blend of sake, garlic, and hot sauce before being set on the grill or under the broiler.

As you can observe from scanning the recipe, this dish is accomplished in two parts. The broiled chicken is the first stanza. The second consists simply of steaming asparagus which are then dressed in Oriental style.

¹/₂	cup plus 1 tablespoon sake (*Japanese rice wine*)
1	small clove garlic, pressed or finely minced
	Dash hot pepper sauce, or to taste
1	pound boneless, skinless chicken breasts, trimmed of all visible fat
1	tablespoon low sodium soy sauce
1	teaspoon sugar
2	teaspoons mild sesame oil
1	tablespoon rice or wine vinegar
¹/₂	teaspoon freshly grated ginger root
1	pound fresh asparagus, trimmed and cut into 2-inch lengths
1	teaspoon fresh lemon juice
1	tablespoon toasted sesame seeds
2	scallions, white and tender greens, thinly sliced

1. In a shallow baking dish, combine ½ cup sake, garlic, and hot pepper sauce. Add chicken, turning to coat on all sides. Cover and refrigerate for at least 1 hour.

2. Preheat broiler or prepare grill.

3. Remove chicken from marinade and grill or broil for about 12 minutes per side or until cooked through but still tender. Tent with foil and set aside briefly.

4. In a small bowl, combine soy sauce, sugar, sesame oil, rice vinegar, and ginger. Whisk well to combine.

5. Steam asparagus until crisp-tender. Toss with soy sauce mixture and set aside.

6. Sprinkle lemon juice over chicken, slice chicken on the diagonal and arrange on a platter interspersed with asparagus. Sprinkle with sesame seeds and scallions and serve warm.

SERVES 4

APPROXIMATELY 175 CALORIES PER SERVING

MADEIRA BRAISED CHICKEN

▶ ▶

This Madeira-laced sauce was frequently the companion of sautéed chicken livers. While I still succumb on very rare occasions, I find tender strips of chicken a worthy substitute.

1/2	cup low sodium chicken broth
4	tablespoons Madeira wine
1	medium clove garlic, chopped
2	tablespoons red wine vinegar
1	tablespoon fresh rosemary or 1 1/2 teaspoons dried
1 1/4	pounds boneless, skinless chicken breasts, trimmed of all visible fat and cut into strips 3/4 inch wide
	Vegetable oil cooking spray
1	teaspoon vegetable oil
1	large shallot, sliced into thin rings
1	tablespoon superfine flour
1/4	cup currants
	Salt and freshly ground pepper to taste

1. In a shallow dish, combine broth, 2 tablespoons Madeira, garlic, vinegar, and rosemary. Add chicken strips, cover, and refrigerate for at least 30 minutes.

2. Heat cooking spray and oil in a nonstick skillet. When hot but not smoking, add shallot and cook over medium heat, stirring, until shallot is well wilted. Remove chicken strips from marinade, reserving marinade, dredge chicken

lightly in flour, and brown quickly. Remove from pan as browned.

3. Pour reserved marinade and remaining Madeira into pan, stir to loosen any browned particles, and simmer over medium-high heat for 2 minutes. Add currants and simmer for 4 to 5 minutes or until liquid is reduced by about half. Taste and add salt and pepper, if desired.

4. Return chicken strips to skillet and stir or shake around in pan to coat with sauce. Serve hot.

SERVES 4
APPROXIMATELY 194 CALORIES PER SERVING

TURKEY BRACCIOLE

▶ ▶

B*racciole* are thin slices of meat or poultry which are rolled around a filling—in this instance, turkey cutlets enclosing a stuffing of sweet red peppers, low fat mozzarella, and fragrant basil.

After browning, the rolls are quickly cooked in a tomato sauce laced with wine, herbs, and a pinch of hot pepper.

3	*teaspoons olive oil*
¹/₂	*medium red bell pepper, trimmed and sliced julienne*
8	*turkey breast cutlets (about 1¹/₄ pounds)*
1	*ounce low fat mozzarella, thinly sliced and cut into strips*
6	*fresh basil leaves, slivered*
2	*cloves garlic, chopped, or to taste*
1	*28-ounce can no-salt-added plum tomatoes, undrained, chopped*
¹/₄	*cup dry white wine*
1	*teaspoon chopped fresh thyme or ¹/₄ teaspoon dried*
1	*teaspoon chopped fresh oregano or ¹/₄ teaspoon dried*
1	*small dried hot red pepper or pinch flakes, or to taste*

1. Heat 1 teaspoon oil in a large nonstick skillet and sauté bell pepper strips over low heat, stirring frequently, for

about 8 minutes or until tender. Remove with a slotted spoon and set aside.

2. Flatten cutlets carefully to an even thickness between 2 pieces of wax paper. Divide red pepper strips, mozzarella, and basil among cutlets. Roll up and secure each with a wooden toothpick.

3. Add remaining 2 teaspoons oil to skillet and brown rolls on all sides. Remove to a warmed plate and tent with foil.

4. Add garlic to skillet and sauté, stirring occasionally, until golden. Raise heat and add tomatoes, wine, herbs, and hot pepper if desired. Cook over medium-high heat for 15 minutes, stirring frequently.

5. Lower heat, return turkey to pan, turning rolls over to coat with sauce, cover, and cook for 5 minutes or until turkey is just cooked through. Serve turkey rolls topped with sauce.

SERVES 4

APPROXIMATELY 258 CALORIES PER SERVING

◆ ◆ ◆ ◆ ◆

TURKEY WITH GARDEN VEGETABLES

▶ ▶

The sensational combination of colors, flavors, and textures makes this one of the best low calorie entrées you can serve. Noodles tossed with a little chicken broth will add to the feeling of well-being already created by this satisfying, healthy affair.

4	turkey breast cutlets (about 1 pound)
1	tablespoon flour
	Vegetable oil cooking spray
1	small shallot, chopped
2	medium carrots, quartered lengthwise and sliced diagonally into 1½-inch pieces
1	large stalk celery, cut in thirds lengthwise and sliced diagonally into 1½-inch pieces
1½	cups clean, sliced fresh mushrooms
½	teaspoon chopped fresh thyme or ¼ teaspoon dried
½	teaspoon chopped fresh tarragon or ¼ teaspoon dried
1	clove garlic, peeled but left whole
1	large ripe tomato, peeled and chopped, or 1 cup canned chopped no-salt-added plum tomatoes, undrained
½	cup dry white wine
¾	cup low sodium beef broth
	Salt and freshly ground pepper to taste

¹/₂ *cup peas, fresh or frozen and thawed*
¹/₄ *cup chopped fresh parsley*

1. Dredge turkey cutlets in flour and shake off excess.

2. Coat a deep, nonstick skillet lightly with cooking spray and place over medium heat. When skillet is hot, add turkey pieces and sear quickly on both sides, then remove from pan and set aside.

3. Add shallot and a little more cooking spray, if necessary, to skillet (remove skillet from heat while adding the additional oil) and sauté shallot until soft, then add remaining ingredients, except peas and parsley, and simmer until vegetables are tender and liquid is reduced by half. Taste and add salt, if desired, and pepper.

4. Return turkey to pan and add peas. Reduce heat, cover, and simmer gently for about 10 minutes or until turkey is cooked through. Stir in parsley and serve.

SERVES 4

APPROXIMATELY 198 CALORIES PER SERVING

♦ ♦ ♦ ♦ ♦

TURKEY FLORENTINE

▶ ▶

This recipe is a variation of a dish made with chicken breasts, skin on, browned in butter, lying on a bed of creamed spinach. Delicious, but packed with calories and other bad things.

In this Good Eating substitute, the butter and cream have been eliminated in favor of a tasty mélange of mushrooms, onions, low fat cheese, and wine-scented spinach.

Olive oil cooking spray

4 turkey breast cutlets (about 5 ounces each)

1/2 cup chopped onion or white part of leek

1 large clove garlic, chopped, or to taste

1/2 pound fresh mushrooms, wiped clean, trimmed, and sliced

1/4 cup low sodium chicken broth

1/2 cup dry white wine

1 1/2 pounds fresh spinach, rinsed, tough stems trimmed

1 ounce low fat Swiss cheese, cut into four strips
Salt and freshly ground pepper to taste
Juice of 1 large lemon

1. Lightly coat a nonstick skillet with cooking spray and brown turkey on both sides over medium-high heat, removing cutlets to a platter as they brown.

2. Add onion or leek, garlic, and mushrooms to skillet, then pour in broth and braise until liquid has evaporated and

mushrooms and onions are tender. Using a slotted spoon, remove vegetables and set aside.

3. Pour wine into skillet and bring to a boil. Add spinach, cover, and cook until well wilted, shaking pan occasionally. Uncover to let excess liquid evaporate, if necessary.

4. Preheat broiler.

5. Transfer spinach to a shallow ovenproof serving dish or casserole. Arrange spinach into 4 equal mounds and top each with a turkey cutlet. Spoon mushroom-onion mixture over turkey, and cover each portion with a strip of cheese. Broil for 3 minutes or until cheese is melted and turkey is heated through. Season with salt and pepper, sprinkle with lemon juice, and serve immediately.

SERVES 4
APPROXIMATELY 242 CALORIES PER SERVING

TURKEY PAPRIKASH

▶▶▶▶▶▶▶▶▶▶▶▶▶▶▶▶▶▶▶▶▶▶▶▶▶▶▶

$\mathbb{P}$aprika is a powder made by grinding red peppers and is closely associated with Hungarian cuisine. It produces a flavor that can range from mild to pungent to hot and has long been used as a last-minute flash of color on a completed dish.

Paprikash refers to paprika-flavored dishes and covers a lot of territory, complementing foods including veal, pork, chicken, and as I've described below, turkey cutlets.

Delicious over broad noodles.

	Vegetable oil cooking spray
6	*turkey breast cutlets (about 1¹/₂ pounds)*
1	*teaspoon vegetable oil*
1	*medium onion, sliced into thin rings*
¹/₂	*pound fresh mushrooms, wiped clean and sliced*
1	*medium green or red bell pepper, seeded and diced*
2	*medium cloves garlic, chopped*
2	*tablespoons mild Hungarian paprika*
2	*tablespoons dry sherry*
1	*bay leaf*
1	*cup low sodium chicken broth*
1	*large ripe tomato, peeled, seeded, and chopped, or 1 cup canned, chopped, no-salt-added tomatoes*
¹/₂	*teaspoon dried savory*
³/₄	*cup low fat (1%) milk*
1	*tablespoon flour*

Salt to taste
1/4 *cup nonfat plain yogurt*
1/4 *cup chopped fresh parsley*

1. Coat a deep nonstick skillet lightly with cooking spray and place over medium heat. When pan is hot, add turkey and brown on both sides. Remove turkey from pan as it browns and set aside.

2. Add oil to skillet, then add onion, mushrooms, and bell pepper and sauté, stirring occasionally or shaking pan, until onion is wilted. Add garlic and sauté for 2 minutes.

3. Stir in paprika and dissolve, then add sherry, bay leaf, broth, tomato, and savory and simmer for 15 minutes or until liquid is reduced by about half.

4. Mix together milk and flour, whisking or stirring until well blended, then stir into skillet. Heat mixture but do not boil. Taste and season with salt, if desired. Return turkey to skillet and cook over low heat for about 5 minutes or until turkey is cooked through and mixture is thickened.

5. Remove skillet from heat. Transfer turkey to a heated serving platter. Stir yogurt and parsley into skillet, spoon sauce over turkey and serve.

SERVES 6
APPROXIMATELY 304 CALORIES PER SERVING

FISH and SHELLFISH

◆ ◆ ◆ ◆ ◆

GRILLED SWORDFISH WITH RED ONION AND MUSHROOM SAUCE

▶▶▶▶▶▶▶▶▶▶▶▶▶▶▶▶▶▶▶▶▶▶▶▶▶▶

The savory sauce in this recipe may serve either as a bed or a topping for the swordfish. The sauce can be prepared in advance, refrigerated, covered, for up to 24 hours, then gently reheated just before serving.

Try this dish with golden polenta and a simple steamed green vegetable.

2	teaspoons olive oil
1	large red onion, cut in half and very thinly sliced
1/2	cup clean, thinly sliced fresh mushrooms
1	cup low sodium chicken broth
2	tablespoons white wine vinegar or dry white wine
1	teaspoon minced fresh oregano or 1/4 teaspoon dried
1	teaspoon minced fresh thyme or 1/4 teaspoon dried
1/4	teaspoon summer savory
	Salt and freshly ground pepper to taste
4	swordfish steaks, about 3/4 inch thick (5 ounces each)
	Olive oil cooking spray

1. Heat oil in a nonstick skillet. Add onion and mushrooms and cook over medium-low heat, stirring often, for 8 to 10 minutes.

2. Add broth and vinegar or wine to skillet, raise heat, and simmer until liquid is reduced by ¼.

3. Prepare grill or preheat broiler.

4. Add oregano, thyme, savory, and salt and pepper to skillet. Simmer gently, stirring occasionally, for 10 minutes. Taste and adjust seasonings, if necessary.

5. Spray swordfish lightly with olive oil on each side and grill or broil for 4 to 5 minutes per side or until just cooked through. Serve with sauce.

SERVES 4

APPROXIMATELY 220 CALORIES PER SERVING

WHOLE TROUT ITALIAN STYLE

▶ ▶

Although designed for trout, this recipe also works well with other small freshwater fish, such as smelt. Small is the operative word here because we're using a skillet rather than broiling or grilling.

On the side, present a bowl of lightly steamed broccoli and cauliflower florets sprinkled with chopped fresh mint.

> 2 teaspoons olive oil
> 4 cloves garlic, coarsely chopped
> 4 whole small trout (about ³/₄ pound each), cleaned, head and tail intact if desired, rinsed and patted dry
> 1 sprig fresh rosemary or ¹/₂ teaspoon dried
> 2 teaspoons minced fresh parsley
>   Salt and freshly ground pepper to taste
>   Juice of 1 large lemon
>   Lemon wedges and parsley sprigs for garnish

1. Heat 1 teaspoon oil in large nonstick skillet over medium-low heat and sauté garlic, stirring often, for about 3 minutes. Do not brown.

2. Add remaining teaspoon oil, trout, rosemary, and minced parsley to skillet. Raise heat to medium and brown fish on both sides. Season with salt and pepper to taste.

3. When fish is browned, add lemon juice and cover skillet lightly. Lower heat and cook for 10-15 minutes or until

fish is just cooked through. Garnish with lemon wedges and parsley sprigs and serve immediately.

SERVES **4**
APPROXIMATELY **203** CALORIES PER SERVING

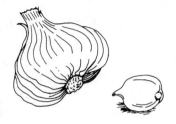

◆ ◆ ◆ ◆ ◆

COD BAKED WITH SWEET PEPPERS

▶▶▶▶▶▶▶▶▶▶▶▶▶▶▶▶▶▶▶▶▶▶▶▶

The white, firm, lean cod is perfectly matched to the onions, garlic, tomatoes, sweet peppers, wine, herbs, and spices with which it stews in the oven. If cod is unavailable, substitute red snapper.

Place the fish on a warm serving platter, leaving space between each steak. Spoon the sweet pepper-tomato mixture between the fish. Try the cod with green noodles or barley and a crisp green salad.

2	teaspoons olive oil
1	large onion, chopped
2	large cloves garlic, chopped
1/2	cup dry white wine
1	cup canned, drained, and chopped no-salt-added tomatoes
1	medium green bell pepper, diced
1	medium red bell pepper, diced
1/4	teaspoon cayenne, or to taste
1	teaspoon fennel seeds
4	cod steaks, 1 inch thick (about 5 ounces each)
1	tablespoon fresh lemon juice

1. Preheat oven to 375°F.

2. Heat oil in a nonstick skillet over medium-low flame and sauté onion and garlic, stirring frequently, until onion is wilted but not browned. Add 1 tablespoon of wine if necessary to keep mixture from sticking.

3. Raise heat to medium and add remaining wine, tomatoes, bell peppers, cayenne, and fennel seeds. Cook for about 10 minutes or until sauce is slightly reduced.

4. Transfer half of sauce mixture to a shallow baking dish, lay in fish steaks, sprinkle with lemon juice, and top with remaining sauce.

5. Bake for 20 minutes or until fish is just cooked through.

SERVES 4
APPROXIMATELY 174 CALORIES PER SERVING

CURRIED HAKE
WITH LIME MARINADE

Ultra low in calories, I serve the curry-fish combination frequently, using hake or another member of the well-populated cod family. Basmati or another long-grain rice and a vegetable round out the meal.

1   tablespoon curry powder
$^1/_8$ teaspoon turmeric
$^1/_8$ teaspoon cayenne (optional if hot curry powder is used)
$^1/_4$ cup plus 2 tablespoons fresh lime juice
2   teaspoons olive oil
4   hake or whiting fillets (about 5 ounces each)
     Salt and freshly ground pepper to taste

1. Combine curry powder, turmeric, cayenne, $^1/_4$ cup lime juice, and oil in shallow baking dish. Place steaks in marinade, turning once to coat. Cover and refrigerate fish for 15 minutes.

2. Preheat broiler.

3. Broil fillets 4 to 5 inches from heat source, basting once or twice with any reserved marinade, for 15 minutes or until fish is just cooked through. Transfer to a heated serving platter, sprinkle with salt, pepper, and remaining lime juice and serve immediately.

SERVES 4

APPROXIMATELY 159 CALORIES PER SERVING

◆ ◆ ◆ ◆

HALIBUT IN A PIQUANT SAUCE

▶ ▶

alibut is considered a relatively lean fish; that is, one that yields about 125 calories per 4-ounce serving before cooking.

Aside from fitting nicely into the low calorie theme of this book, halibut is one of the more flavorful members of the flounder family. And, with the notable exception of grilling, it takes to a wide variety of cooking methods.

Serve with steamed, lightly glazed baby carrots.

> 1 *pound halibut fillets*
> 1 *tablespoon sesame oil*
> 4 *scallions, white and tender greens, sliced*
> 2 *tablespoons dry sherry*
> 1 *cup canned low sodium chicken broth*
> 1 *tablespoon low sodium soy sauce*
> 2 *tablespoons rice vinegar or cider vinegar*
> 1 *teaspoon sugar*
> 1 *tablespoon fresh lemon juice*
> 1/2 *pound Swiss chard or young Chinese cabbage*
>   (*bok choy*), *trimmed and rinsed*

1. Rinse halibut, pat dry, cut into large, bite-size pieces, and set aside.

2. Heat oil in large nonstick skillet and sauté scallions over medium heat for 5 minutes or until wilted and beginning to brown.

3. Add sherry, 1/4 cup broth, and fish pieces. Cook, shaking pan frequently, for about 4 minutes.

4. Add remaining ingredients, except Swiss chard or cabbage, and simmer for 5 minutes or until slightly reduced.

5. While sauce reduces, boil or steam Swiss chard or bok choy until just wilted. Drain greens and spread out on a heated serving platter.

6. Arrange fish over greens, pour sauce over fish, and serve.

SERVES 4

APPROXIMATELY 184 CALORIES PER SERVING

COHO SALMON
STEAMED IN SPINACH BLANKETS

◆▶▶▶▶▶▶▶▶▶▶▶▶▶▶▶▶▶▶▶▶▶▶▶◀

This spectacular dish is perfect for small dinner parties or as a special show-off dish for the family.

As a variation, wrap the salmon in broad-leaf lettuce or napa cabbage leaves. Virtually guilt-free, this main course can be served with boiled diced beets or turnip-potato puree and a big, splashy salad.

10 to 12	*large spinach leaves, well rinsed, tough stems trimmed*
2	*tablespoons nonfat plain yogurt*
2	*teaspoons Dijon mustard*
2	*teaspoons fresh lemon juice*
1½	*tablespoons plus 2 teaspoons minced fresh dill weed*
	Salt and freshly ground pepper to taste
1	*pound coho salmon fillets, all visible bones plucked with tweezers, divided into four servings*

1. Place a few spinach leaves at a time in very hot water and let stand for 1 or 2 minutes or until wilted. Repeat until all spinach has been softened.

2. In a small bowl, combine yogurt, mustard, lemon juice, 1½ tablespoons dill, and salt and pepper to taste. Stir to blend ingredients thoroughly.

3. Make spinach blankets by laying out 2-3 spinach leaves (depending on the size of the leaves), overlapping

them slightly to make a blanket big enough to wrap completely around a salmon fillet. Mound 1/4 of the yogurt mixture in the center of each spinach blanket and spread until the spinach is coated to within 1/2 inch of edges with the sauce. Place 1 serving of salmon over the sauce on each spinach blanket and sprinkle with 1/2 teaspoon of the remaining dill. Wrap spinach leaves around fish to enclose completely. Repeat procedure until all 4 fillets are bundled.

4. Place wrapped fillets seam side down in a steamer, cover and steam for 5 or 6 minutes or until just tender. Do not overcook.

SERVES 4
APPROXIMATELY 188 CALORIES PER SERVING

◆ ◆ ◆ ◆

SALMON FILLETS
WITH LEEK PUREE

▶ ▶

Here, salmon fillets are broiled and served over a luxurious leek puree, seasoned with tomato paste, broth, and thyme. Lemon slices and sprigs of fresh thyme make lovely plate decorations.

3/4	cup low sodium chicken broth
2	medium leeks, white and about 1 inch of greens, well rinsed and chopped
2	teaspoons tomato paste
1/2	teaspoon chopped fresh thyme or 1/4 teaspoon dried
	Salt and freshly ground pepper to taste
1	pound salmon fillets, divided into four servings
3	tablespoons dry white wine
2	tablespoons fresh lemon juice
	Lemon slices and thyme sprigs for garnish

1. Heat 1/4 cup broth in a large nonstick skillet over medium heat. Add leeks and cook, stirring often, for 8 minutes or until well wilted.

2. Add tomato paste and stir until well blended. Add remaining broth and thyme and raise heat slightly. Cook mixture for 4 minutes or until slightly reduced.

3. Transfer contents of skillet to a food processor and puree. Taste and add salt and pepper, if needed.

4. Preheat broiler.

---

5. Place salmon fillets in a large baking dish and spoon wine and lemon juice over. Broil, about 4 or 5 inches from heat source, for 6 to 8 minutes or until fish is springy to the touch but not flaky (broiling time will depend on thickness of fillets).

6. If necessary, reheat puree and spoon onto 4 warmed plates. Gently lift salmon with spatula and lay over puree. Garnish with lemon slices and sprigs of fresh thyme and serve.

SERVES 4

APPROXIMATELY 206 CALORIES PER SERVING

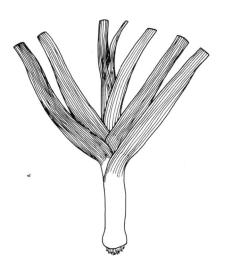

◆ ◆ ◆ ◆ ◆

RED SNAPPER VERA CRUZ
(Adapted from Zapata)

▸ ▸

I used to frequent a little neighborhood Mexican restaurant in New York City called Zapata. But, when Wall Street crashed, many Manhattan dwellers fled the high-priced co-ops, condos, and rising apartment rents. Unfortunately, so did many of the commercial renters and leasers. As a result, some terrific local shops and restaurants had to close their doors permanently. Zapata was one of those caught in the ebbing tide of the economy.

In its heyday, though, Zapata served a number of exemplary Mexican dishes. Among my favorites was their *Huachinago a la Veracruzana*, that is, Red Snapper Vera Cruz Style. Fortunately, I cajoled Pancho (yes, Pancho!), the cook, into sharing his delicious recipe which I have adapted to a Good Eating life-style and am delighted to share here.

4	*red snapper fillets (about 5 ounces each)*
1/4	*cup fresh lemon or lime juice*
3	*tablespoons water, approximately*
2	*medium onions, chopped*
2	*medium cloves garlic, sliced*
1	*tablespoon capers, rinsed and drained*
6	*pitted green olives, rinsed and drained*
1	*tablespoon dry sherry*
1/2	*teaspoon chili powder*
1/4	*teaspoon dried oregano or marjoram*

$^1/_8$ teaspoon ground cinnamon
Pinch ground cloves
2 sprigs fresh parsley, chopped
2 cups no-salt-added tomato puree
2 pimientos, sliced lengthwise into strips
Salt and freshly ground pepper to taste
Lime wedges for garnish

1. Rub both sides of fish with lemon or lime juice and refrigerate for 15 to 20 minutes.

2. Heat a large nonstick saucepan over medium flame, add water and onions and simmer until onions are softened. Add garlic and additional water, if necessary, and cook until water has evaporated and onion is golden.

3. Preheat oven to 350°F.

4. Add remaining ingredients, except pimientos, fish, and salt and pepper to saucepan. Cook over medium heat, stirring occasionally, for 15 minutes or until sauce is slightly thickened and flavors are blended.

5. Place the fish in an ovenproof casserole in a single layer, sprinkle with salt and pepper and pour sauce over. Cover and bake for 20 minutes or until fish is tender. Top with pimiento and garnish with lime wedges.

SERVES 4
APPROXIMATELY 217 CALORIES PER SERVING

BROILED MAHIMAHI
IN SHALLOT CREAM SAUCE

◆◆◆◆

▶▶▶▶▶▶▶▶▶▶▶▶▶▶▶▶▶▶▶▶▶▶▶

Mahimahi is a variety of dolphin fish—do not become hysterical. Dolphin fish is NOT kin to Flipper, who was a porpoise and therefore a mammal. Dolphin fish is a fish.

Mahimahi is a lean fish that cooks rather quickly. So keep your eye on it as it broils. Touch it. Learn the feel of done fish. It will have a "give"—a slight springy resistance—when it is done.

Here, the mahimahi is treated to a sauce consisting of sautéed shallots, Worcestershire, bourbon, wine, and a last-minute fling with light sour cream. Accompany the dish with your favorite grain, from bulgur to barley to quinoa to kasha, or with boiled tiny red or new potatoes and a brisk spinach salad.

    4   mahimahi steaks (about 5 ounces each)
        Vegetable oil cooking spray
    2   teaspoons olive oil
    6   medium shallots, minced
    1   teaspoon Worcestershire sauce
    1/4 cup bourbon
    3/4 cup white wine
    1/4 cup light sour cream
        Salt and freshly ground pepper to taste
    4   parsley sprigs for garnish

1. Preheat broiler.
2. Place mahimahi in a shallow baking pan lightly

coated with cooking spray. Broil about 4 inches from heat source for 5 to 6 minutes per side or until just cooked through.

3. While fish broils, heat oil in a nonstick skillet. Add shallots and sauté over medium heat for 3 minutes or until shallots start to soften. Reduce heat, add Worcestershire sauce and cook, stirring, for an additional minute.

4. Add bourbon and wine, raise heat to high and stir until sauce starts to boil. Remove from heat and stir in sour cream. Taste and add salt and pepper, if needed.

5. Transfer broiled fish to a heated serving platter. Pour sauce over fish, garnish with parsley and serve immediately.

SERVES 4
APPROXIMATELY 180 CALORIES PER SERVING

◆ ◆ ◆ ◆ ◆

TUNA WITH YELLOW PEPPER SAUTÉ

▶ ▶

T ry this delightful combination of colors and textures over linguine or spaghetti squash with a salad of lettuces drizzled with a rambunctious vinaigrette sauce.

3	teaspoons olive oil
1½	cups coarsely chopped yellow bell pepper
1	small red onion, thinly sliced
2	cloves garlic, minced
3	ripe plum tomatoes, chopped
¼	cup bottled clam juice
2	tablespoons dry red wine
6	pitted black olives, thinly sliced crosswise
½	tablespoon chopped fresh rosemary or 1 teaspoon dried
	Salt and freshly ground pepper to taste
4	tuna steaks, 1 inch thick (about 5 ounces each)

1. Preheat oven to 400°F.

2. Heat 2 teaspoons oil in large saucepan over medium heat. Add yellow pepper, onion, and garlic and sauté, stirring often, for 3 to 5 minutes or until onion and pepper are softened.

3. Add tomatoes, clam juice, wine, olives, rosemary, and salt and pepper and bring to a boil. Cook, stirring frequently, for 8 minutes or until thickened.

4. Meanwhile, brush tuna steaks with remaining teaspoon oil. Heat an ovenproof skillet until hot but not smoking.

Sear tuna over high heat for 30 to 45 seconds per side or until lightly browned.

5. Transfer skillet to oven and bake for about 10 minutes or until flesh is opaque. Remove from oven, top with tomato mixture and serve.

SERVES 4
APPROXIMATELY 236 CALORIES PER SERVING

SEA SCALLOPS
IN GARLICKY MARINARA SAUCE

◆◆◆◆◆

▶▶▶▶▶▶▶▶▶▶▶▶▶▶▶▶▶▶▶▶▶▶▶

Not since King Kong lovingly cradled Fay Wray in his mammoth hands has there been a more magnetic union of opposites: the assertive with the diffident; the powerful with the delicate; the bountiful with the beautiful; garlic with scallops.

To serve, transfer to deep soup plates and offer crusty bread for dunking, along with a crisp salad. Or you may prefer to feast on the scallops marinara as the sauce over your favorite long-stranded pasta.

2	teaspoons olive oil
1	small onion, finely chopped
3	large cloves garlic, minced
1	28-ounce can no-salt-added crushed tomatoes
1/4	cup dry red wine
1/2	cup chopped fresh Italian parsley
	Dash hot pepper sauce, or to taste
1	teaspoon dried marjoram or oregano
1	bay leaf
	Salt and freshly ground pepper to taste
1	pound sea scallops, large scallops cut in half

1. Heat oil in a large saucepan and sauté onion and garlic over medium heat, stirring, until garlic is just golden.

2. Raise heat, add tomatoes, wine, 1/4 cup parsley, hot sauce, marjoram, bay leaf, and salt and pepper to taste. Cook over medium-high heat, stirring often, for 5 minutes.

3. Add scallops, cover, and continue cooking, shaking the pan frequently, for about 6 minutes or until scallops are just cooked through.

4. Remove from heat, taste sauce and correct seasonings, if necessary. Transfer to a heated platter, sprinkle with remaining parsley, and serve immediately.

SERVES 4
APPROXIMATELY 176 CALORIES PER SERVING

◆ ◆ ◆ ◆

SHRIMP IN THE SHELL
WITH LEMON OREGANO DRESSING

▶ ▶

This dressing, reminiscent of *salmoriglio*, the Italian lemon-oil-herb mixture, has only a fraction of the oil but enough zing to serve with almost any fish or shellfish.

If you can get them, fresh herbs make a subtle but delicious difference in this dish.

1¹/₂	tablespoons olive oil
¹/₄	cup fresh lemon juice
1	teaspoon water
1	garlic clove, halved
1	tablespoon chopped fresh oregano or 1 teaspoon dried
1	tablespoon chopped fresh parsley or 1 teaspoon dried
1	small dried hot red pepper pod, uncracked
	Salt to taste
16	jumbo shrimp in shell (*about 1 pound*)

1. Preheat broiler or prepare grill.

2. Combine all ingredients, except shrimp, and let stand at room temperature while shrimp are prepared. (Dressing can be made in advance and refrigerated for 24 hours. Return to room temperature before serving.)

3. Cut shrimp along back to devein, but do not remove shell. Rinse shrimp well.

4. Grill or broil shrimp for 4 minutes per side or just until thoroughly pink.

5. Transfer cooked shrimp to warmed serving dishes. Remove hot pepper pod and garlic halves from dressing and spoon an equal amount of sauce over each portion.

SERVES 4
APPROXIMATELY 171 CALORIES PER SERVING

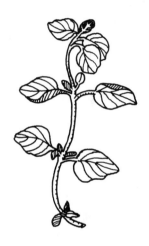

◆ ◆ ◆ ◆ ◆

BAKED SHRIMP
WITH TOMATOES AND FETA

▶▶▶▶▶▶▶▶▶▶▶▶▶▶▶▶▶▶▶▶▶▶

Because feta—the Greek cheese traditionally made from sheep's or goat's milk—is cured and generally packed in brine, there is no need for added salt in this recipe. Although used in small quantities (about one tablespoon per serving), the tangy flavor of feta will make its presence known and appreciated in this luscious "dish from Hellas." The fragrant dill adds a special touch.

    2   teaspoons olive oil
         Olive oil cooking spray
    4   scallions, white and tender greens, chopped
    2   whole cloves garlic, flattened
  1/8   teaspoon dry mustard
  1/4   teaspoon sugar
    1   28-ounce can no-salt-added plum tomatoes,
         undrained, chopped
   24   large shrimp (about 1 pound), peeled and
         deveined
  1/4   cup rinsed, drained, and crumbled feta cheese
    2   tablespoons minced fresh parsley
    1   tablespoon minced fresh dill weed or 1/2
         tablespoon dried

1. Heat oil and cooking spray in a large nonstick skillet and sauté scallions and garlic over medium-low heat until onions are translucent and garlic is lightly golden. If garlic

begins to brown, remove from pan with a slotted spoon and discard.

2. Stir in mustard, blending well, and then add sugar. Raise heat to medium-high and add tomatoes and their juice. Stir to blend well and cook for 15 minutes.

3. Meanwhile, preheat oven to 425°F.

4. Place shrimp in a shallow baking pan. Spoon sauce over shrimp, top with crumbled feta, and sprinkle with fresh parsley and dill. Bake, uncovered, for 15 minutes or until shrimp is cooked through and cheese is softened.

SERVES **4**

APPROXIMATELY **210** CALORIES PER SERVING

♦ ♦ ♦ ♦ ♦

CAJUN CRAB CAKES
(Adapted from Carole Welch)

▶ ▶

Crab cakes are to the Bayou what bubbles are to champagne. Every stop you hit—from elegant restaurants to roadside juke joints—serves its own special blend. Of course, these dynamite patties can range from the divine to the dreadful. Every cook, crook, and granny, it seems, has a recipe and shape they call their own. Some like them round and light like Ping-Pong balls. Others prefer them flat and dense like discus. I must be perverse, because I like them all—that is, as long as their prime ingredient is crabmeat.

I borrowed this recipe from my friend Carole the Caterer who says she purloined it from a New Orleans chef friend of hers. I've adapted it to accommodate the spirit of our low-cal life-style.

Try these cakes accompanied by Remoulade Sauce (page 14).

> Vegetable oil cooking spray
> 1   medium stalk celery, cut in pieces
> 1   small red bell pepper, seeded and cut in pieces
> 2   large shallots or ¹/₂ medium onion, quartered
> 1   large clove garlic, quartered
> ¹/₂ cup fresh bread crumbs, preferably made from day-old French bread
> 2   large egg whites, lightly beaten
> 1   teaspoon Dijon mustard
> ¹/₂ teaspoon paprika

$^1/_2$ teaspoon cayenne, or to taste
   Salt and freshly ground pepper to taste
1 pound cooked crabmeat, fresh or frozen, picked
   over and flaked
   Parsley sprigs and lemon wedges for garnish

1. Preheat oven to 350°F. Coat a baking sheet lightly with cooking spray and set aside.

2. Combine celery, bell pepper, shallot or onion, and garlic in a food processor and process until finely chopped but not pureed. Transfer mixture to a mixing bowl.

3. Add bread crumbs, egg whites, mustard, paprika, cayenne, and salt and pepper to bowl and mix well. If mixture is too dry to hold together, add water, 1 tablespoon at a time. Add crab and stir just to blend.

4. Shape mixture into 8 balls, flatten each ball into a patty about $^3/_4$-inch high, and place patties on prepared baking sheet. Bake in upper third of oven for 20 minutes, turn cakes and bake an additional 15 minutes or until golden and slightly crispy outside. Serve 2 cakes per person, garnished with parsley sprigs and lemon wedges.

SERVES 4
APPROXIMATELY 166 CALORIES PER SERVING

♦ ♦ ♦ ♦ ♦

SAFFRON SEAFOOD STEW

▶ ▶

Ideal for small parties or larger groups, this dish has the aura of complexity and refinement that belies its simplicity.

Serve with a mixed green salad and toasted French bread rounds rubbed lightly with garlic.

1¹/₂	cups low sodium chicken broth
¹/₂	cup dry white wine
¹/₂	cup bottled clam juice
¹/₂	cup apple juice
1	tablespoon fresh lemon juice
1	medium stalk celery, diced
1	medium onion, diced
1	medium carrot, diced
1	large potato, peeled and cubed
2	teaspoons minced fresh parsley or 1 teaspoon dried
1	teaspoon dried tarragon
¹/₂	teaspoon dried dill weed
¹/₂	teaspoon crumbled saffron threads, or to taste
³/₄	pound sole or flounder fillets
2	dozen littleneck clams, scrubbed
12	sea scallops, cut in half
18	large shrimp (about ³/₄ pound), shelled and deveined
	Salt and freshly ground pepper to taste
2	tablespoons half-and-half

1. In a large stockpot, combine broth, wine, and juices and bring to a boil. Reduce heat and add celery, onion, carrot, potato, parsley, tarragon, dill, and saffron. Cover and simmer over low heat, stirring occasionally, for 20 minutes.

2. Add fish and seafood, raise heat to medium, cover and simmer, stirring occasionally, for about 8 minutes or until fish is opaque and the clams have opened.

3. Using a slotted spoon, remove fish, seafood (discarding any unopened clams), and large pieces of vegetables from pot and arrange in 6 heated bowls.

4. Taste liquid in pot and add salt and pepper, if needed. Cook over high heat for about 5 minutes or until liquid is reduced by $1/3$. Remove from heat and stir in half-and-half. Spoon liquid over fish and vegetables in bowls and serve.

SERVES 6

APPROXIMATELY 246 CALORIES PER SERVING

PIZZAS
and
PASTA
SAUCES

◆ ◆ ◆ ◆ ◆

BASIC PIZZA CRUST

▶ ▶

Use this crust for the pizza recipes that follow, or create your own toppings. If you prefer a whole-wheat crust, use 1 cup whole-wheat flour and 1½ cups all-purpose flour. Don't be afraid to experiment. And if you indulge in pizza often, a pizza stone for the oven is a great investment.

> 1   cup warm water (about 115°F.)
> 1   package active dry yeast
> 2   teaspoons olive oil
> 2½ cups all-purpose flour, approximately
> ¼   teaspoon salt
>   Vegetable oil cooking spray
> 1   tablespoon cornmeal

1. Pour water into a large warmed bowl. Sprinkle with yeast and stir to dissolve. Let stand about 5 minutes. Add oil, 1½ cups flour, and salt, and stir; dough should be sticky. Add remaining flour, a little at a time, until dough is workable and no longer sticky (at some point you will have to stop stirring with a spoon and start using your hands).

2. Turn dough out onto a lightly floured surface and knead for 5 minutes or until dough is smooth. Clean the work bowl and coat it lightly with cooking spray. Shape dough into a ball and place in the bowl, turning over once to coat the dough with a film of oil. Cover the bowl with a clean kitchen towel and let stand in a warm place, free of drafts, for about 45 minutes or until dough has doubled in bulk (if you press

two fingers about ¹/₂ inch into the dough and the indentations remain, it has risen enough).

3. Punch the dough down with your fist (it will deflate rather suddenly), peel it out of the bowl, and divide dough into two halves. (At this point dough can be formed into two balls, and frozen, well wrapped in plastic. Defrost in the refrigerator and then return to room temperature before continuing with recipe.)

4. Roll one ball of dough out into a thin circle, ideally 12 inches round (or roll into a rectangle to fit a baking sheet, approximately 10- by 15-inch). Coat a 12-inch pizza pan or baking sheet with cooking spray, sprinkle surface with cornmeal, and fit dough to edges of pan (gently push from center to edge of dough to stretch it out if necessary).

5. Add toppings and bake (usually in a preheated 500°F. oven for about 15 minutes).

MAKES CRUST FOR TWO 12-INCH-DIAMETER (OR 10- BY 15-INCH) PIES
APPROXIMATELY 1,138 CALORIES PER SINGLE CRUST
APPROXIMATELY 190 CALORIES PER SLICE (¹/₆ CRUST)

◆ ◆ ◆ ◆ ◆

PIZZA PRIMAVERA

▶ ▶

A slightly lighter version of the traditional Margherita pizza, with a topping of fresh vegetables.

Dough for 1 pizza crust (see Basic Pizza Crust, page 133)

- 2 *teaspoons olive oil*
- 1 *large clove garlic, chopped*
- 2 *cups canned, drained and chopped no-salt-added plum tomatoes*
Salt and freshly ground pepper to taste
- ¹/₄ *teaspoon hot red pepper flakes, or to taste*
- 6 *thin stalks asparagus, tough stalks ends removed, sliced diagonally*
- 1 *cup broccoli florets*
- ³/₄ *cup low fat ricotta cheese*
- ¹/₂ *cup clean, thinly sliced fresh mushrooms*
- ¹/₄ *cup freshly grated Parmesan or Romano cheese*
- 6 *fresh basil leaves, coarsely shredded*

1. Prepare pizza crust through step 4. Preheat oven to 500°F.

2. Heat oil in large nonstick skillet over medium-low heat and sauté garlic until softened. Raise heat to high and add tomatoes (they will splatter). When tomatoes boil, reduce heat slightly, add several grindings of pepper, a pinch of coarse salt if desired, and hot pepper flakes, and cook for about 10 minutes, stirring occasionally (can be made ahead and refrigerated or frozen).

3. While sauce cooks, steam asparagus and broccoli to the crisp-tender stage.

4. Spoon tomato sauce into center of pizza and spread gently toward edges, leaving about a ³/₄-inch border of dough. Drop teaspoonfuls of ricotta on top of tomato sauce, arrange asparagus, broccoli florets, and mushrooms over surface, then sprinkle top with Parmesan and basil shreds.

5. Bake for 15 minutes on the bottom rack of the oven or until crust is golden and cheese is bubbly. Remove from oven and let sit 2 minutes before serving.

MAKES ONE 12-INCH PIZZA
APPROXIMATELY 259 CALORIES PER SLICE (¹/₆ PIZZA)

◆ ◆ ◆ ◆ ◆

PIZZA WITH TURKEY SAUSAGE AND ROASTED PEPPERS

▶▶▶▶▶▶▶▶▶▶▶▶▶▶▶▶▶▶▶▶▶▶▶▶▶

You can substitute unroasted peppers and the flavor will be different, but no less delicious (for instructions on roasting peppers, see page 21).

> *Dough for 1 pizza crust (see Basic Pizza Crust, page 133)*
>
> 1   *teaspoon olive oil*
>   *Vegetable oil cooking spray*
> 3   *ounces Italian-flavored turkey sausage, casings removed*
> 1   *medium onion, sliced into thin rings*
> ¹/₄ *cup dry red wine*
> ³/₄ *cup no-salt-added crushed tomatoes*
> 1   *teaspoon sugar*
> ¹/₂ *teaspoon dried oregano or marjoram*
>   *Freshly ground pepper to taste*
> 1   *small red bell pepper, roasted and cut into thin strips*
> 1   *small green bell pepper, roasted and cut into thin strips*
> 6   *large black olives, rinsed, drained, pitted, and halved*
> 3   *tablespoons freshly grated Parmesan cheese*

1. Prepare pizza crust through step 4.

2. Heat oil and cooking spray in a nonstick skillet and sauté turkey sausage over medium heat, stirring to break up

large clumps, until mixture begins to brown. Add onions and sauté until well wilted (add a tablespoon or so of the wine if necessary).

3. Raise heat and add remaining wine, cook for 1 minute, then add tomatoes all at once. Sprinkle with sugar, oregano, and several grindings of pepper and cook for about 10 minutes. Remove from heat and cool to room temperature.

4. Meanwhile, preheat oven to 500°F.

5. Spoon tomato mixture into center of dough and spread out over dough, leaving about a ¾-inch border. Lay roasted pepper strips and olives over sauce and sprinkle with Parmesan.

6. Bake on bottom rack of preheated oven for 15 minutes or until crust is golden and topping bubbles. Remove from oven and let sit for about 5 minutes before slicing and serving.

MAKES ONE 12-INCH PIZZA
APPROXIMATELY 288 CALORIES PER SLICE (⅙ PIZZA)

ARTICHOKE PIZZA WITH MOZZARELLA AND SMOKED TURKEY

▶ ▶

This white pizza (made without tomatoes) also works well with all manner of colorful sliced vegetables. Don't be afraid to experiment, but be sure to include the calorie counts for any additions.

Dough for 1 pizza crust (see Basic Pizza Crust, page 133)
Olive oil cooking spray
1/2 cup low fat ricotta cheese
1 teaspoon dried Italian herb blend
Freshly ground pepper to taste
2 ounces smoked turkey breast, slivered
3/4 cup thickly sliced artichoke hearts, canned in water or frozen and thawed
1/4 cup rinsed, drained, and sliced black olives
1 1/2 ounces low fat mozzarella, cut into small pieces

1. Prepare pizza crust through step 4. Preheat oven to 500°F.

2. Spray a thin layer of oil over the top of the crust, leaving about a 1-inch border of dough.

3. Spread ricotta thinly around the crust and sprinkle with herb blend and pepper to taste. Scatter smoked turkey slivers, artichoke heart slices, olives, and mozzarella over pizza.

4. Bake in preheated oven for 15 minutes or until topping is bubbly and crust is golden. Remove pizza from oven and let stand a few minutes before slicing.

MAKES ONE 12-INCH PIZZA
APPROXIMATELY 254 CALORIES PER SLICE (¹/₆ PIZZA)

PESTO PIZZA
WITH SUN-DRIED TOMATO SAUCE

▶ ▶

The combination of intensely flavored sun-dried tomatoes and fragrant basil give this pizza an incredible zing.

> Dough for 1 pizza crust (see Basic Pizza Crust, page 133)
>
> 2 cups firmly packed fresh basil
>
> 1 cup firmly packed fresh parsley
>
> 8 sun-dried tomato halves (not oil-packed), soaked in boiling water for 5 minutes, drained, and chopped
>
> 1 small onion, chopped
>
> 3 cloves garlic, chopped
> Freshly ground pepper to taste
>
> 1/2 cup grated Parmesan cheese
>
> 1/4 cup low sodium chicken broth
>
> 2 tablespoons olive oil
>
> 2 ripe plum tomatoes, thinly sliced
>
> 1/4 cup minced fresh basil or parsley

1. Prepare pizza crust through step 4. Preheat oven to 500°F.

2. Combine basil, parsley, sun-dried tomatoes, onion, garlic, pepper, and 1/4 cup grated cheese in food processor or blender and process for 5 seconds or until ingredients are thoroughly combined. With motor running, add broth, then oil in a slow, steady stream.

3. Spoon sauce into center of pizza and spread gently toward edges, leaving about a ³/₄-inch border of dough. Arrange tomato slices over sauce, sprinkle with minced basil or parsley and drizzle with remaining cheese.

4. Bake in preheated oven for 15 minutes or until crust is golden.

5. Remove pizza from oven, and let stand for 2 or 3 minutes before slicing.

MAKES ONE 12-INCH PIZZA
APPROXIMATELY 264 CALORIES PER SLICE (¹/₆ PIZZA)

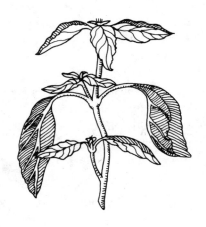

◆ ◆ ◆ ◆ ◆

MANHATTAN CLAM PIZZA

▶ ▶

A unique and delicious pizza, made without cheese.

> *Dough for 1 pizza crust (see Basic Pizza Crust, page 133)*
> 1½ *dozen littleneck clams, shucked and chopped or 10-ounce can whole clams, drained and chopped*
> 2 *cups canned, drained, chopped no-salt-added plum tomatoes*
> 4 *cloves garlic, minced*
> 3 *tablespoons chopped fresh parsley*
> ¼ *cup dry white wine*
> 1 *cup thinly sliced onion rings or 1 large leek, chopped*
> 1 *tablespoon chopped fresh oregano or 1 teaspoon dried*
> 1 *tablespoon chopped fresh tarragon or ½ teaspoon dried*
> *Freshly ground pepper to taste*
> *Olive oil cooking spray*

1. Prepare pizza crust through step 4.

2. Combine clams with tomatoes, garlic, parsley, wine, onion slices, oregano, and tarragon. Refrigerate for 30 minutes. Meanwhile, preheat oven to 500°F.

3. With a slotted spoon, remove clam and tomato mixture from bowl and spread over the top of the dough, leaving about a ¾-inch uncovered border. If topping seems dry, add a few tablespoons of juice left in the bowl. Do not allow pie to

---

become too soggy. Sprinkle with generous grindings of pepper and add a light top coating of cooking spray.

4. Bake in preheated oven for 15 minutes or until crust is golden and topping is bubbly. Remove from oven and let stand a few minutes before slicing.

MAKES ONE 12-INCH PIZZA
APPROXIMATELY 235 CALORIES PER SLICE (¹/₆ PIZZA)

◆ ◆ ◆ ◆ ◆

GOAT CHEESE PIZZA
WITH RED AND YELLOW PEPPERS

▶ ▶

The distinctive flavor and creamy texture of goat cheese in concert with sweet bell peppers and seasonings guarantees you'll get plenty of requests for this recipe. I sometimes divide the ingredients into 6 individual pizzas. They make a gorgeous addition to any hors d'oeuvres table.

> Dough for 1 pizza crust (see Basic Pizza Crust, page 133)
> Olive oil cooking spray
> 1/2 cup crumbled mild goat cheese (about 4 ounces)
> 1 large shallot, very thinly sliced into rings
> 1 clove garlic, finely minced
> 1 small red bell pepper, seeded and cut into strips
> 1 small yellow bell pepper, seeded and cut into strips
> 1/4 cup slivered, loosely packed fresh basil
> Freshly ground pepper to taste
> 1/4 cup freshly grated Parmesan cheese
> 1/4 teaspoon crumbled saffron threads (optional)

1. Prepare pizza crust through step 4. Preheat oven to 500°F.

2. Spray crust lightly with cooking spray, then sprinkle goat cheese thinly over the top, leaving about a 1-inch border uncovered. Arrange shallot rings, garlic, bell pepper strips, and basil slivers on top of cheese. Top with two or three

---

grindings of pepper, grated Parmesan, and saffron. Finish with another light coating of cooking spray.

3. Bake pizza in preheated oven for 15 minutes or until crust is golden and toppings are wilted and bubbly. Remove from oven and let rest a few minutes before serving.

MAKES ONE 12-INCH PIZZA
APPROXIMATELY 275 CALORIES PER SLICE (¹⁄₆ PIZZA)

♦ ♦ ♦ ♦ ♦

PASTA SAUCES

▶ ▶

For the sauces that follow, I have indicated approximately how many portions each recipe will serve. Although specific types of pasta are named, these are suggestions only. Feel free to substitute your favorite pasta or grain.

Calorie counts are for sauces only. Uncooked pasta is approximately 105 calories per ounce.

♦ ♦ ♦ ♦ ♦

SHRIMP AND OLIVE SAUCE FOR CAPELLINI

▶ ▶

Lost beneath heavier sauces, capellini shines through in this light, olive-scented creation.

   Olive oil cooking spray
2 *teaspoons olive oil*
1 *small onion, diced*
1 *clove garlic, minced*
³/₄ *pound medium shrimp, shelled and deveined*
4 *large ripe tomatoes, coarsely chopped*
¹/₄ *cup rinsed, drained, and sliced black olives*
¹/₄ *cup minced fresh basil*

1 tablespoon minced fresh Italian parsley
Salt and freshly ground pepper to taste

1. Bring pasta water to a boil.
2. Heat cooking spray and oil in a large nonstick skillet. Add onion and garlic and cook over medium heat for 3 minutes or until onion is translucent.
3. Add shrimp, tomatoes, olives, and basil to skillet and cook over medium heat, stirring often, for 3 to 5 minutes or until shrimp just turn pink.
4. As soon as you add the shrimp to the skillet, slide pasta into boiling water and cook until al dente.
5. Drain pasta and toss with shrimp mixture, parsley, and salt and pepper to taste. Divide among warmed pasta bowls and serve.

SERVES 4
APPROXIMATELY 157 CALORIES PER SERVING

◆ ◆ ◆ ◆ ◆

VEGETABLE SAUCE FOR ORZO

▶ ▶

Orzo, a small, rice-shaped pasta, is an interesting alternative but feel free to substitute your favorite pasta variety.

> 1 cup low sodium chicken broth
> 1 teaspoon olive oil
>   Vegetable oil cooking spray
> 1 medium onion, chopped
> 1 large clove garlic, chopped
> 1 medium carrot, diced
> 1 medium stalk celery, diced
> 1 small yellow bell pepper, cut in julienne strips
> 2 medium fresh, ripe tomatoes, diced, juice reserved
> 1/4 cup fresh basil, torn in pieces or slivered
>   Freshly ground pepper to taste

1. In a small saucepan, heat broth to boiling, adjust heat until mixture simmers and cook until reduced by about half. Remove saucepan from heat and cover.

2. Heat olive oil in a large nonstick skillet or kettle coated lightly with cooking spray. Add onion and sauté over medium heat, stirring occasionally, until wilted. Add garlic and cook for an additional 2 minutes.

3. Stir in carrot, celery, yellow pepper, and tomatoes with their juice. Cook for about 10 minutes, stirring occasionally.

4. Meanwhile, cook pasta in boiling, salted water until just tender.

5. Add broth to vegetable mixture and bring to a simmer. Drain pasta thoroughly and add to skillet along with basil. Toss quickly and divide among warmed pasta bowls. Pass peppermill separately.

SERVES 4

APPROXIMATELY 60 CALORIES PER SERVING

◆ ◆ ◆ ◆ ◆

SUMMER SAUCE

▶ ▶

T he perfect way to use leftover ears of cooked fresh sweet corn, combined with plump ripe summer tomatoes and fragrant basil. Wagon wheel pasta creates an interesting, if somewhat fanciful, presentation.

2 teaspoons olive oil
1 large clove garlic, chopped
2 large ripe tomatoes, cubed, juice reserved
2 medium ears corn, raw or cooked, kernels cut from cobs
8 fresh basil leaves, torn into large pieces
   Salt and freshly ground pepper to taste

1. Slide pasta into boiling water.

2. While pasta cooks, heat oil in a large nonstick skillet and sauté garlic over low heat for about 2 minutes or until softened. Raise heat to medium, add tomatoes with juice, and cook until just bubbling. Add corn, reduce heat to medium-low, and cook until corn is heated through.

3. Drain pasta and add to skillet. Add basil and salt and pepper to taste. Toss or stir quickly, just to combine. Serve hot.

SERVES 4
APPROXIMATELY 75 CALORIES PER SERVING

◆ ◆ ◆ ◆ ◆

GORGONZOLA SAUCE
FOR FETTUCCINE

▶ ▶

Although only a small amount of blue cheese is used, the heady flavor shines through in this creamy, rich-tasting sauce. While I usually toss this with spinach fettuccine, a refreshing alternative would be cooked spaghetti squash.

    ¹/₄   cup low sodium chicken broth
    1   small clove garlic, chopped
    1   cup low fat (1%) cottage cheese
    1¹/₂ ounces gorgonzola or other blue cheese, crumbled
    4   tablespoons grated Parmesan cheese
    ¹/₄   cup chopped scallion greens
    3   tablespoons white wine vinegar
          Freshly ground pepper to taste

1. Slide pasta into boiling water.

2. Heat one tablespoon broth in a nonstick skillet and sauté garlic over medium heat until lightly golden.

3. Combine cheeses, scallion greens, remaining broth, and vinegar in a food processor and blend until smooth.

4. Remove skillet from heat and beat in cheese mixture. Taste and add ground pepper, if desired. Reduce heat to very low and return skillet to flame. Heat briefly.

5. Drain pasta well and quickly add to skillet. Toss until pasta is well coated and serve immediately.

SERVES 4
APPROXIMATELY 114 CALORIES PER SERVING

◆ ◆ ◆ ◆ ◆

PORCINI CREAM SAUCE

▶▶▶▶▶▶▶▶▶▶▶▶▶▶▶▶▶▶▶▶▶▶▶▶▶▶▶

D ried porcini mushrooms are available in most specialty or gourmet shops and some larger supermarkets. Because porcini have such a unique and intense flavor, substituting white mushrooms simply will not yield the same results. Serve with broad linguine or penne.

1	ounce dried porcini mushrooms
¹/₂	cup very warm water
1	cup low sodium beef broth
¹/₄	teaspoon dried thyme
¹/₄	teaspoon dried rosemary
1	tablespoon diet margarine
¹/₂	cup finely diced celery
1	medium leek, white bulb only, chopped
1¹/₂	cups clean, sliced white mushrooms
2	tablespoons flour
³/₄	cup low fat (1%) milk
2	tablespoons minced fresh parsley

1. Cover porcini mushrooms with warm water and set aside for 45 minutes. Chop mushrooms and reserve ¹/₄ cup of the soaking liquid.

2. Combine broth and dried herbs in a small saucepan and reduce liquid to ¹/₂ cup over medium-high heat.

3. Heat margarine in a large nonstick skillet over medium heat and sauté celery and leek until softened, stirring occasionally. Add chopped porcinis and white mushrooms

and sauté until mushrooms are tender. Meanwhile, slide pasta into boiling water.

4. Sprinkle mixture in skillet with flour, stirring to dissolve, then raise heat and add reduced broth and reserved soaking liquid. Cook, stirring, until mixture comes to a simmer. Remove skillet from heat and stir in milk. Reduce flame to very low and return skillet to stove. Cook, stirring, until thickened, but do not boil.

5. Drain pasta and toss with sauce, divide among warmed pasta bowls, sprinkle with parsley and serve hot.

SERVES 4
APPROXIMATELY 99 CALORIES PER SERVING

◆ ◆ ◆ ◆ ◆

SPICY SAUSAGE BOLOGNESE

▶ ▶

Originating in Bologna, Italy, the classic version of this ragu is made with fatty ground beef or veal. Substituting lower fat Italian-flavored turkey sausage and lightening up on the oil makes this dish affordable in calories and outstanding in flavor. This sauce is best with a sturdy pasta such as rigatoni.

$1/2$	cup chopped onion
1	clove garlic, chopped
$1/2$	cup low sodium chicken broth
$1/2$	medium carrot, chopped
$1/2$	medium stalk celery, chopped
1	small red bell pepper, seeded and chopped
$1/4$	pound fresh mushrooms, wiped clean, trimmed, and chopped or sliced
$1/4$	pound hot Italian-flavored turkey sausage, casings removed
$1/2$	cup dry white or red wine
$1/3$	cup low fat (1%) milk
2	cups chopped, canned, no-salt-added plum tomatoes, undrained
$1/4$	teaspoon fennel seeds
$1/4$	teaspoon dried oregano or thyme
	Salt and freshly ground pepper to taste
2	tablespoons chopped fresh parsley
4	tablespoons freshly grated Romano cheese (optional at 23 calories per tablespoon)

1. Braise onion and garlic in 1/4 cup broth until onion is softened, then add remaining broth, carrots, celery, bell pepper, and mushrooms and cook over medium heat for 6 to 8 minutes or until vegetables are just tender and liquid is nearly evaporated.

2. Crumble turkey sausage into pan and cook, stirring and breaking up large clumps, just until sausage loses its raw color. Do not brown.

3. Raise heat, pour in wine, and cook, shaking pan occasionally, until liquid has evaporated. Remove from heat and stir in milk, then return pan to low heat and cook, stirring, until milk is absorbed.

4. Add tomatoes, fennel seeds, and oregano, raise heat, and bring mixture to a boil. Reduce heat to very low and cook for about 45 minutes, stirring from time to time. Taste and add salt and pepper, if desired. (Sauce can be made ahead and refrigerated or frozen.)

5. Cook pasta to desired degree of doneness and drain well. Reheat sauce, if necessary, and toss with pasta, parsley, and cheese if desired. Serve hot.

SERVES 4

APPROXIMATELY 102 CALORIES PER SERVING WITHOUT CHEESE

POACHED TUNA
AND VEGETABLE SAUCE

▶ ▶

Serve this robust sauce with a sturdy pasta such as rotelli or ziti.

2	cups water
1	small onion, sliced
1	tablespoon whole black peppercorns
2	tuna steaks, 1 inch thick (about 4 ounces each)
2	teaspoons olive oil
2	cloves garlic, flattened
1	small onion, chopped
1	tablespoon tomato paste
1	28-ounce can no-salt-added plum tomatoes in puree
1/2	cup full-bodied red wine
2	teaspoons dried oregano
1	teaspoon dried thyme
1	cup broccoli florets
1/2	cup sliced yellow summer squash
1/2	cup sliced zucchini
1/2	cup clean, sliced mushrooms
	Salt and freshly ground pepper to taste

1. In a deep skillet, heat water with sliced onion and peppercorns until boiling. Cook for 5 minutes, then reduce heat to low and add tuna steaks. Cover and poach gently for 10 minutes or until fish is cooked through. Remove tuna from

skillet and set aside to cool, discarding liquid with onions and peppercorns.

2. Heat oil in large nonstick skillet or saucepan and sauté garlic and onion over medium-low heat, stirring often, for 5 minutes or until onion is translucent.

3. Raise heat and stir in tomato paste. Cook for 2 minutes, stirring often, then add tomatoes, chopping them with a large spoon in the pan. Add wine, sprinkle with herbs, and bring to a boil. Reduce heat to medium and cook sauce, stirring occasionally, for 30 minutes.

4. Add broccoli, squash, zucchini, and mushrooms. Cover and simmer for 20 minutes or until vegetables are tender. Stir in salt if desired, and pepper.

5. When sauce is nearly ready, cook pasta until just slightly firm to the bite.

6. Drain pasta, toss well with sauce and vegetables, and divide among warmed plates. Cut tuna into chunks and arrange on top.

SERVES 6
APPROXIMATELY 113 CALORIES PER SERVING

VEGETABLES and GRAINS

◆ ◆ ◆ ◆ ◆

RED POTATOES IN
PARSLEY SHALLOT SAUCE

▶▶▶▶▶▶▶▶▶▶▶▶▶▶▶▶▶▶▶▶▶▶▶▶▶▶▶

An ideal accompaniment to any grilled or broiled lean meat or fowl.

1¹/₄	pounds small red potatoes, well scrubbed
2	teaspoons olive oil
2	medium shallots, minced
1	scallion, white and tender greens, finely minced
1	small clove garlic, minced
¹/₂	bunch fresh parsley, well trimmed and chopped (about 1³/₄ cups)
¹/₂	cup fresh bread crumbs
¹/₂	teaspoon mild Dijon mustard (optional) Salt and freshly ground pepper to taste

1. Boil unpeeled potatoes until just tender (cooking time will vary according to size of potatoes).

2. While potatoes cook, heat oil in nonstick skillet. Add shallots, scallion, and garlic and sauté over medium-low heat for 5 minutes or until wilted. Stir in parsley, bread crumbs, and mustard if desired, and sauté, stirring frequently, until bread crumbs are golden. Season with salt and pepper.

3. Drain potatoes, cut into halves and toss with parsley mixture while potatoes are still very hot. Serve immediately.

SERVES 6
APPROXIMATELY 103 CALORIES PER SERVING

◆ ◆ ◆ ◆ ◆

TWICE-BAKED
SPICED SWEET POTATOES

▶ ▶

I was served the original of this flavorsome side dish at a Thanksgiving dinner, but when I asked the hostess for her recipe, she concluded by saying, ". . . and loads of butter and heavy cream." After a little experimenting, I came up with this low fat adaptation which eliminates the butter and cream but retains the sweet and spicy taste.

2	sweet potatoes, scrubbed
	Vegetable oil cooking spray
$^1/_2$	teaspoon ground ginger
$^1/_2$	teaspoon ground nutmeg
$^1/_2$	teaspoon ground allspice
$^1/_2$	teaspoon ground coriander
	Salt and freshly ground pepper to taste
4	teaspoons firmly packed brown sugar
$^3/_4$	cup evaporated low fat milk

1. Preheat oven to 400°F.

2. Pierce the potatoes several places to allow steam to escape. Bake for 45 minutes or until potatoes are tender. Remove from oven, let stand until cool enough to handle, and cut in half lengthwise. Reduce oven temperature to 350°F.

3. Carefully scoop out pulp from potatoes, leaving shells intact, and transfer pulp to a mixing bowl. Place shells, cut side up, on a baking sheet coated with cooking spray and set aside.

4. Sprinkle ginger, nutmeg, allspice, coriander, salt, pepper, and 2 teaspoons brown sugar over potato pulp and mash to blend. Add milk and mash or whisk until ingredients are thoroughly combined.

5. Divide pulp mixture among the 4 potato shells, smoothing tops with the back side of a spoon, and sprinkle each with ½ teaspoon of remaining brown sugar.

6. Return to oven and bake for 15 minutes. Serve immediately.

SERVES 4

APPROXIMATELY 133 CALORIES PER SERVING

◆ ◆ ◆ ◆ ◆

ROASTED BABY ROOT VEGETABLES

▶ ▶

H ardier and more dense by nature, root vegetables such as turnips and beets offer sweet and colorful winter fare. I love them in soups, stews, purees, sauces, and roasted in the oven.

In this recipe the fire does all the work, aside from very basic preparation, and the entire process should take under an hour from start to finish. Roasted vegetables look (and taste) terrific alongside just about any entrée you have planned on your menu. I even adore them stuffed between two pieces of textured bread, drizzled with a hint of good, fruity olive oil.

> 12 *baby carrots, scraped and trimmed*
> 16 *pearl onions, peeled*
> 12 *baby or 4 medium turnips, peeled, trimmed,*
> *scrubbed, large turnips cut in thirds*
> 12 *baby or 6 medium red beets, peeled, trimmed,*
> *scrubbed, large beets cut in half horizontally*
> *Olive oil cooking spray*
> *Salt and freshly ground pepper to taste*
> 2 *tablespoons chopped fresh thyme or 1 tablespoon*
> *dried*
> 2 *tablespoons chopped fresh parsley*

1. Preheat oven to 375°F.

2. Bring 1 cup water to boil in a saucepan, add carrots, blanch for 1 minute, then drain.

3. Place carrots and remaining vegetables in a single

layer in a shallow roasting pan lightly coated with cooking spray. Spray vegetables lightly with olive oil, season with salt, if desired, and pepper, and sprinkle with thyme if using dried. Roast for 45 minutes or until vegetables are tender and beginning to brown. Transfer to a heated platter, sprinkle with parsley and fresh thyme, if used, and serve.

SERVES 6
APPROXIMATELY 61 CALORIES PER SERVING

◆ ◆ ◆ ◆

MADRAS TOMATO AND OKRA CURRY

▶ ▶

This is a semi-dry dish and goes well with white rice and meat or fish. A nice accompaniment is cucumber with yogurt and mint.

1	tablespoon vegetable oil
1	teaspoon mustard seeds
2	large onions, finely chopped
4	cloves garlic, minced
1/2	teaspoon hot red pepper flakes, or to taste
1	teaspoon freshly minced ginger root
1	teaspoon turmeric
1/2	teaspoon ground cumin
4	large ripe tomatoes, finely chopped, juice reserved
4	ounces okra, preferably baby or young okra, slit lengthwise in half
3	tablespoons water
	Salt to taste

1. Heat oil in a wide nonstick skillet and sauté mustard seeds over medium heat, shaking the skillet occasionally. When they begin to snap, add the onions, garlic, hot pepper flakes, and ginger, and sauté for 2 minutes. Add the turmeric and cumin and stir well.

2. Add tomatoes and juice and simmer over medium heat for about 5 minutes. Add okra and water, stir well, and

continue cooking for 10 minutes, adding additional water by the tablespoonful if needed. Taste and add salt, if desired.

SERVES 4
APPROXIMATELY 126 CALORIES PER SERVING

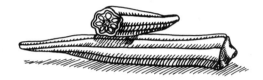

◆ ◆ ◆ ◆ ◆

CHILLED WINTER VEGETABLES
IN LEMON VINAIGRETTE

▶ ▶

I can't imagine a lovelier still life than this bouquet created from marinated winter vegetables set in a bowl on the dining table.

This dish would be a vivacious addition to any pasta, plain broiled, grilled, or sautéed fish, fowl, or meat entrée.

> 1/3 cup fresh lemon juice
> 1 tablespoon minced fresh parsley
> 1 tablespoon minced fresh basil or 1 teaspoon dried
> 1 tablespoon minced fresh oregano or 1 teaspoon dried
> 2 teaspoons olive oil
> 1 medium clove garlic, coarsely chopped
> Salt and freshly ground pepper to taste
> 2 large carrots, sliced diagonally into 1-inch pieces
> 8 Brussels sprouts
> 1/2 cup cauliflower florets
> 1/2 cup broccoli florets
> 1/2 cup cherry tomatoes

1. Combine lemon juice, parsley, basil, oregano, oil, and garlic in a jar with a tight lid. Shake well to blend, then taste and add salt and pepper.

2. Steam carrots for 5 to 8 minutes or until crisp-tender. Remove carrots from steamer, reserving water. Rinse carrots in cold water and set aside.

3. Discard tough outer leaves of Brussels sprouts and cut

small slashes in the bottoms. Steam sprouts in reserved water for 3 minutes. Add cauliflower and continue cooking for another 5 minutes. Remove vegetables from steamer, reserving water. Rinse vegetables under cold water and set aside.

4. Steam broccoli for 5 minutes, rinse under cold water and set aside.

5. Combine steamed vegetables with cherry tomatoes and toss with vinaigrette. Cover and refrigerate for 8 hours or overnight.

SERVES 4
APPROXIMATELY 59 CALORIES PER SERVING

◆ ◆ ◆ ◆

ASPARAGUS
WITH ASPARAGUS SAUCE

▶ ▷

A dream come true for asparagus lovers!

1¹/₂	*pounds asparagus*
¹/₃	*cup low sodium chicken broth*
1	*teaspoon olive oil*
1	*tablespoon fresh lemon juice*
1	*teaspoon dry mustard*
	Salt and freshly ground pepper to taste
2	*hard-cooked egg whites, chopped*
2	*teaspoons capers, rinsed and drained*

1. Rinse asparagus and snap off and discard the tough lower portion of stems. Reserving 4 stalks, set remaining asparagus aside.

2. Place the 4 asparagus stalks in a saucepan with enough water to cover and bring to a boil. Lower heat slightly, cover, and simmer for 12 minutes or until asparagus is very tender. Drain, cut into pieces and transfer to a food processor.

3. Steam remaining asparagus until crisp-tender, about 8 minutes if stalks are thick.

4. While asparagus steams, prepare sauce. Add broth, oil, lemon juice, mustard, and salt and pepper to food processor with asparagus stalks. Process until smoothly pureed.

5. Arrange steamed asparagus on individual serving

plates and spoon an equal amount of asparagus sauce over each portion. Top each serving with a sprinkling of chopped egg whites and a ½ teaspoon of capers.

SERVES 4

APPROXIMATELY 37 CALORIES PER SERVING

GREENS AND BEANS

▶ ▶

I like to think of this wonderful dish as a kind of low-cargo cassoulet or a hearty escarole with beans soup. At any rate, this combo should be a featured player in any Mediterranean-style menu. You can enhance the taste and reduce the sodium even further if you use freshly cooked beans.

1	teaspoon olive oil
1	medium shallot, chopped
2	large cloves garlic, chopped, or to taste
1	cup low sodium beef broth or bouillon
1	tablespoon red wine vinegar
1½	pounds escarole (about 1 large head), trimmed, well rinsed, and drained
2	cups cooked or canned, rinsed and drained white kidney (cannellini) beans
	Freshly ground pepper to taste

1. In a large, deep skillet, heat oil and sauté shallot over medium heat for 3 minutes. Add garlic and cook, stirring, until garlic begins to turn pale gold.

2. Raise heat to high and pour in broth. Cook until reduced by about ¼ cup. Add vinegar and stir briefly to blend.

3. Add escarole in layers, leaving pieces whole. Reduce heat, cover, and cook at a bare simmer until escarole begins to wilt. Lay beans gently on top of greens, replace cover and

continue to simmer until greens are well wilted and beans are heated through. Add fresh pepper to taste and serve hot.

SERVES 6
APPROXIMATELY 85 CALORIES PER SERVING

◆ ◆ ◆ ◆ ◆

SWEET AND TART EGGPLANT

▶ ▶

This heavenly eggplant/black currant quiniela is a real winner for low-cal gourmets and is perfect with almost any mildly flavored meat or fowl.

Because vinegar will vary in strength and acidity, it's important to adjust the amount called for in the recipe according to the vinegar you use most frequently at home.

¹/₄	*cup dried black currants*
¹/₄	*cup semi-dry white wine*
2	*teaspoons olive oil*
1	*red onion, thinly sliced*
1	*small clove garlic, minced*
1	*large eggplant, unpeeled, diced*
¹/₄	*cup red wine vinegar, approximately*
1	*tablespoon sugar*
2	*tablespoons chopped fresh parsley*
2	*tablespoons chopped fresh mint or 1 tablespoon dried*
	Salt and freshly ground pepper to taste

1. Combine currants and wine in a small saucepan and bring to a boil. Remove saucepan from heat and let currants sit in wine until softened while the rest of the dish is prepared.

2. Heat oil in large nonstick skillet and sauté onion over medium heat until wilted. Add garlic and sauté for an additional 2 minutes. Add eggplant and cook, stirring, for about 10 minutes or until eggplant is tender. Transfer eggplant mixture to a bowl. Do not wipe skillet.

3. Drain currants, reserving wine, and add currants to eggplant mixture.

4. Add reserved wine, vinegar, and sugar to skillet. Cook over medium heat, stirring, until sugar dissolves. Return eggplant mixture to skillet along with parsley, mint, and salt and pepper to taste. Raise heat to high and cook for 2 minutes. Serve hot or at room temperature.

SERVES 4
APPROXIMATELY 93 CALORIES PER SERVING

◆ ◆ ◆ ◆ ◆

GREEN AND YELLOW
BEANS BALSAMIC

▶ ▶

I s this a warm salad? Is it a vegetable dish? The answer is Both! And it's great no matter what you call it. Steamed green and yellow beans may be served hot, warm, or at room temperature, and with just about anything.

¹/₂	*pound green beans, ends trimmed*
¹/₂	*pound yellow (wax) beans, ends trimmed*
1	*teaspoon olive oil*
	Olive oil cooking spray
2	*shallots, minced*
2¹/₂	*tablespoons balsamic vinegar*
2	*tablespoons low sodium chicken broth*
1	*teaspoon coarse-grained mustard*
2	*tablespoons minced fresh parsley*
	Salt and freshly ground pepper to taste

1. Steam green and yellow beans for about 5 minutes or until crisp-tender. Drain and refresh quickly under cold water.

2. Heat oil in a large nonstick skillet coated with cooking spray and sauté shallots over medium heat until very wilted and just beginning to brown.

3. Add vinegar, broth, and mustard to skillet. Stir to blend ingredients and simmer for about 1 minute. Add drained beans and parsley and cook for another 2 minutes,

---

stirring or shaking pan often. Sprinkle with salt and pepper
and serve.

SERVES 4
APPROXIMATELY 55 CALORIES PER SERVING

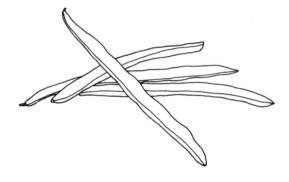

◆ ◆ ◆ ◆ ◆

BRAISED COLLARD GREENS
(Adapted from The Boondocks)

▶ ▶

Some years ago there existed a jazz club all the way on the west side of New York City, near the Hudson River, on about 18th or 19th Street. It was called—I kid you not—The Boondocks. And there was never a place more appropriately named. "The Boonies" was a soul-food restaurant of some repute. It could be said that both the musicians and the kitchen cooked! Herewith is a rendition of one of their best selections, braised collard greens.

If you prefer, substitute mustard or turnip greens—it won't significantly affect the caloric content of the finished dish.

1	bunch collard greens (about 1½ pounds)
1	teaspoon peanut oil
1	clove garlic, chopped
½	cup low sodium chicken broth
1	teaspoon dry mustard
1	teaspoon white vinegar
	Salt and freshly ground pepper to taste
	Pinch cayenne, or to taste

1. Wash greens well under running water. Trim and discard stems and tough ribs. Shred, chop, or cut leaves into bite-size pieces.

2. Heat oil in a large nonstick skillet. Add garlic and cook for 2 minutes. Add broth, mustard, vinegar, salt and pepper, and cayenne if desired. Stir over medium heat until

blended, then add collard greens, cover, and steam for 10 to 15 minutes or until collards are tender.

    3. Transfer greens to a heated platter and serve.

SERVES **4**

APPROXIMATELY **51** CALORIES PER SERVING

◆ ◆ ◆ ◆ ◆

CARROT PUREE

▶ ▶

Here is a low-cal version of one of my most cherished favorites. I stopped eating it whipped with butter and warmed heavy cream a long time ago. Now, I devour it often and without the least bit of guilt.

> 4 *medium carrots, cut into 1-inch slices*
> 1 *medium potato, peeled and cubed*
> 1 *small onion, quartered*
>   *Salt and freshly ground pepper to taste*
> 1 *teaspoon sugar*
> 1/4 *cup evaporated low fat milk*
>   *Vegetable oil cooking spray*

1. Preheat oven to 400°F.

2. Combine carrots, potato, and onion in a large saucepan. Add enough water to cover (lightly salted, if desired), and bring to a boil. Cover, adjust heat, and simmer for 15 minutes or until vegetables are tender.

3. Drain vegetables well and transfer to a food processor (it may be necessary to do this in batches; if so, divide ingredients equally). Add salt and pepper, sugar and milk, and process until smoothly pureed.

4. Transfer mixture to a small baking dish lightly coated with cooking spray and bake for 10 minutes or until lightly browned on top.

SERVES 4

APPROXIMATELY 82 CALORIES PER SERVING

◆ ◆ ◆ ◆ ◆

CABBAGE WITH CARAWAY

▶ ▶

Caraways are those pesky little devils that always seem to find their way to the infinitesimally small spaces between the teeth. But, I so love these tiny terrors that I've somehow learned to redirect their route to a more manageable area of my mouth.

Caraways are the aromatic seeds of an herb in the parsley family. Their wonderfully nutty, vaguely anise flavor has long made them a favorite in the cuisines of Germany, Austria, and Hungary where they're used both to scent and flavor everything from breads and cakes to cheese, stews, meats, and vegetables. The cabbage preparation below is but one example of their versatility and contribution to the character of a dish.

Cabbage with Caraway is excellent with roasts and grilled or poached poultry and is terrific in an all-vegetarian dinner that might include mashed or baked potatoes, Twice Baked Spiced Sweet Potatoes (page 162), baked acorn squash, or your favorite recipe for grain.

2   teaspoons unsalted margarine
1   small head green cabbage (about 1 pound), cored and coarsely shredded
1   clove garlic, minced
    Salt and freshly ground pepper to taste
2   tablespoons cider vinegar
1   teaspoon sugar
1   teaspoon caraway seeds

1. Heat margarine in a large nonstick skillet with a tight lid. Add cabbage, garlic, and salt and pepper to taste. Stir well over medium heat for about 2 minutes or until ingredients are blended and cabbage is coated with margarine. Cover tightly, reduce heat slightly, and steam for 10 minutes or until cabbage is tender.

2. Add remaining ingredients and mix well. Serve immediately.

SERVES 4

APPROXIMATELY 49 CALORIES PER SERVING

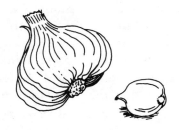

◆ ◆ ◆ ◆ ◆

BULGUR WITH CURRANTS

▶▶▶▶▶▶▶▶▶▶▶▶▶▶▶▶▶▶▶▶▶▶▶▶▶

For a change, try this Mideast favorite instead of rice.

1	teaspoon olive oil
1	small onion, finely chopped
1	cup coarse or medium uncooked bulgur
2	cups hot low sodium chicken broth
1/4	cup currants
	Salt and freshly ground pepper to taste

1. Preheat oven to 350°F.

2. In a 3-quart ovenproof casserole, heat oil over medium flame. Add onion and sauté, stirring frequently, for about 5 minutes or until onion is softened but not browned. Add bulgur and sauté, stirring constantly, until bulgur is well coated.

3. Add broth and currants, stir, and bring to a boil. Cover and transfer pot to oven. Bake for 45 minutes or until liquid has been absorbed and bulgur is tender. Do not stir during this time. Taste and adjust seasonings, if desired. Fluff the bulgur with two forks and serve.

SERVES 4
APPROXIMATELY 161 CALORIES PER SERVING

QUICK PAELLA VALENCIANO

▶ ▶

his festive and hearty adaptation is a meal unto itself.

1	teaspoon olive oil
	Olive oil cooking spray
1	medium onion, chopped
4	cups low sodium chicken broth
1¹/₂	cups uncooked white rice
2	boneless, skinless chicken breast halves (about ¹/₂ pound), trimmed of all visible fat and cubed
2	sprigs parsley, chopped
¹/₄	teaspoon crumbled saffron threads, or to taste
	Salt and freshly ground pepper to taste
1	pound large shrimp, peeled and deveined
2	dozen littleneck clams, scrubbed
1	cup green peas, fresh or frozen and thawed
¹/₄	cup diced pimientos
6	pitted black olives, rinsed, drained, and sliced

1. Heat oil in a large stockpot coated with cooking spray and sauté onion over medium-high heat, stirring often, for about 4 minutes or until onion begins to brown.

2. Add broth and bring to a boil. Lower heat, stir in rice, and add chicken, parsley, saffron, and salt and pepper to taste. Cover and simmer slowly for 20 minutes.

3. Add shrimp, clams, peas, pimientos, and olives, and continue cooking, covered, for an additional 10 minutes or until rice is tender (check liquid occasionally—the paella

---

should not be soupy, but if too much liquid has evaporated, add water by the tablespoonful).

4. Discard any unopened clams, and serve paella on a heated platter.

SERVES 6
APPROXIMATELY 369 CALORIES PER SERVING

◆◆◆◆◆
MUSSELS RISOTTO

▶▶▶▶▶▶▶▶▶▶▶▶▶▶▶▶▶▶▶▶▶▶▶▶▶▶

Risotto requires vigilance during cooking, but it's well worth it.

> 2 cups water
> 1/2 cup dry white wine
> 2 dozen mussels, well scrubbed and debearded
> 1 cup low sodium chicken broth
> 1/4 teaspoon crumbled saffron threads (optional)
>   Salt and freshly ground pepper to taste
> 2 teaspoons olive oil
> 1 medium onion, finely chopped
> 1 large garlic clove, minced
> 1 cup uncooked Arborio rice or short-grain white rice
> 2 tablespoons chopped fresh parsley
>   Freshly ground pepper to taste

1. Bring water and wine to a boil in a large pot. Add mussels, cover and steam until shells open, 5 to 7 minutes. Using a slotted spoon, remove mussels to a colander, discarding any that have not opened, and reserve cooking liquid. Remove mussels from shells and set aside. Discard shells.

2. Strain cooking liquid and return to pot. Add broth, saffron, and salt and pepper to taste. Heat until simmering, then adjust heat to keep liquid at a slow simmer.

3. Heat oil in a large nonstick skillet. Add onion and garlic and sauté over medium heat for 5 minutes or until golden.

---

4. Add rice to skillet and stir well to coat with onion mixture.

5. Stir simmering broth mixture, 1/2 cup at a time, into the rice in skillet, and cook over medium heat, stirring constantly and allowing rice to absorb the liquid before adding any more. Continue adding heated liquid, 1/2 cup at a time, and cook for about 20 minutes or until rice is creamy.

6. Add mussels to skillet, stir in parsley and pepper, and serve hot.

SERVES 4

APPROXIMATELY 345 CALORIES PER SERVING

DESSERTS

RICOTTA CHEESECAKE
WITH FRESH RASPBERRY SAUCE

▶ ▶

In my experience, some brands of low fat ricotta cheese have more moisture than others. If the ricotta has a visible amount of liquid on top when you open the container, pour off liquid before proceeding with the recipe.

The rosewater adds a subtle, distinctive flavor (rosewater is available at specialty and health-food stores, or in cosmetic departments—use only rosewater which specifies that it can be used for confections, not toilet water with alcohol or chemicals). If it is not readily available to you, it may be left out.

	Vegetable oil cooking spray
2	15-ounce containers low fat ricotta cheese
	Thawed frozen egg substitute equal to 3 whole eggs
1/2	cup evaporated low fat milk
1/2	cup low fat buttermilk
1/2	cup plus 2 tablespoons sugar
1 1/2	teaspoons vanilla extract
2	teaspoons rosewater (optional)
1	tablespoon orange juice
1	tablespoon coarsely chopped, toasted almonds
1	tablespoon grated orange zest

RASPBERRY SAUCE
1	pint fresh raspberries, picked over and rinsed

1½   tablespoons fresh lemon juice
1   tablespoon kirsch (optional)
1   teaspoon superfine sugar

1. Preheat oven to 375°F. Lightly coat a 9-inch spring-form pan with cooking spray and set aside.

2. In the bowl of a food processor, combine cheese, egg substitute, milk, buttermilk, sugar, vanilla extract, rosewater, and orange juice. Blend well, scraping down sides several times if necessary. Stir in almonds and orange zest and transfer batter to prepared pan (batter will be slightly thin).

3. Bake in center of oven for 45 minutes or until center no longer jiggles. Cake will pull away from sides slightly.

4. While cake bakes, prepare sauce by combining berries with remaining sauce ingredients in a food processor; process briefly, until berries are coarsely pureed. Strain seeds, if desired.

5. Cool cake completely on rack before removing sides of pan, and serve with raspberry sauce.

SERVES 10
APPROXIMATELY 153 CALORIES PER SERVING CAKE
APPROXIMATELY 15 CALORIES PER TABLESPOON SAUCE

◆ ◆ ◆ ◆ ◆

SPICED APPLE PEAR CRISP

▶ ▶

Apples and pears pop up most often in the familiar double-crust pies. Crisps, such as the one I've outlined below, are also a showcase for these two delectable autumn fruits.

Basically, a crisp is nothing more than fruit baked with a crumbly flour, sugar, and fat (in this case diet margarine) topping. It's as simple to make as it is scrumptious to eat. Serve warm.

	Vegetable oil cooking spray
¹/₂	cup all-purpose unbleached flour
¹/₄	cup whole-wheat flour
¹/₃	cup packed light brown sugar
1	teaspoon ground ginger
¹/₂	teaspoon ground coriander
¹/₂	teaspoon ground allspice
¹/₄	cup rolled oats
3	tablespoons diet margarine
2	large or 3 small just-ripe pears
3	large apples, preferably McIntosh
	Juice of 1 large lemon
2	tablespoons thawed frozen apple juice concentrate

1. Preheat oven to 375°F. Coat an 8-inch-square baking pan lightly with cooking spray and set aside.

2. Combine flours with brown sugar and spices. Add oats and margarine and cut in just until mixture resembles coarse crumbs. This can be done in a food processor with one

or two pulsing motions (do not overblend; mixture should be very grainy). Set aside.

3. Peel, core, and slice apples and pears, tossing with lemon juice as soon as they are sliced to keep them from discoloring.

4. Layer apple and pear slices into pan. Sprinkle with apple juice concentrate and then with flour mixture. Bake ½ hour or until topping is crisp and filling is bubbly.

SERVES 8
APPROXIMATELY 179 CALORIES PER SERVING

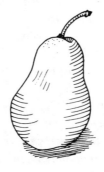

♦ ♦ ♦ ♦

FROZEN GRAPES
WITH CINNAMON YOGURT
(Adapted from Rick Young)

▶ ▶

Some years ago, my friend Rick Young worked at an advertising agency as an account executive. His job description included heavy client contact—which meant he had to suffer fools gladly: that is, entertain them. Rick would be a missing person most lunch hours—on business, of course—at restaurants, entertaining clients. Poor thing, he also found himself in the company of clients at his home, where he and his dutiful wife would "do a barbecue" or a buffet for the benefit of guests.

Rick's heightened sense of survival (and expediency) led him to devise this easy yet elegant dessert, which has become a favorite at my house. The original recipe called for sour cream, but I find yogurt to be a wise substitute. Besides, everyone I know appreciates being exposed to a little more culture, especially when it tastes this good.

1½   *pounds seedless green grapes, rinsed and removed
       from stems*
1   *cup nonfat vanilla yogurt*
2   *teaspoons ground cinnamon*
1   *teaspoon sugar*
      Mint sprigs for garnish

1. Pat grapes dry, transfer to a plastic bag and put in the freezer for about 2 hours or until frozen. (Grapes can be kept

frozen for up to 3 days.) Remove from freezer and pour grapes into a chilled serving dish.

2. In a small mixing bowl, combine yogurt, cinnamon, and sugar. Pour over frozen grapes and toss gently to coat. Serve immediately garnished with mint.

SERVES 6
APPROXIMATELY 113 CALORIES PER SERVING

◆ ◆ ◆ ◆

BUTTERMILK POPPYSEED CHIFFON CAKE

▶ ▶

No egg yolks, no whole milk, no butter makes this cake a great low fat, low-cal option. Vanilla, lemon, poppyseeds, and other goodies make it delicious. And, as an added bonus, this simple, homey cake will take care of itself while other foods are cooking or other work is being done.

Vegetable oil cooking spray
2   teaspoons plus 1¹/₂ cups sifted cake flour
1¹/₄ cups plus 2 tablespoons sugar
2   teaspoons baking powder
1   teaspoon baking soda
2   tablespoons poppyseeds
¹/₄   teaspoon salt
7   large egg whites, at room temperature
¹/₄   teaspoon cream of tartar
¹/₃   cup safflower oil
¹/₃   cup warm water
¹/₃   cup low fat buttermilk
1¹/₂ teaspoons vanilla extract
3   tablespoons fresh lemon juice
1   tablespoon grated lemon zest

1. Preheat oven to 350°F. Coat a 9-inch bundt pan lightly with cooking spray and sprinkle with 2 teaspoons flour. Shake out excess flour and set pan aside.

2. In a small bowl, sift together remaining flour, 1¹/₄ cups sugar, baking powder and soda, poppyseeds, and salt.

3. In a large, grease-free bowl, beat egg whites until frothy. Add cream of tartar and beat until soft peaks form. Add remaining 2 tablespoons sugar and beat until stiff but not dry.

4. Add oil, water, buttermilk, vanilla extract, lemon juice, and lemon zest to flour mixture and stir just to combine. In three batches, add buttermilk mixture to egg whites, folding gently with a spatula.

5. Pour batter into prepared pan and bake in center of preheated oven for 45 minutes or until tester inserted in center of cake comes out clean. (Note that this cake remains pale in color. Don't assume that it isn't done. Test it anyway.) Remove from oven and cool 15 minutes on a rack, then invert onto a plate and cool completely before serving.

SERVES 12
APPROXIMATELY 195 CALORIES PER SERVING

◆ ◆ ◆ ◆ ◆

PROFITEROLES
WITH CHOCOLATE SAUCE
(Adapted from Margaret Sullivan)

▶ ▶

This is a three-part dessert, and each part can be made and enjoyed separately. You can fill the profiteroles with frozen yogurt, ice milk, or fresh berries. If you omit the sugar (and the requisite calories), the puffs can be baked and filled with a light chicken or shrimp salad. The crème pâtisserie custard can be served with a fruit sauce or used in a tart crust, and the sauce can be spooned over pound cake, ice milk, or whatever.

Of course, the combination—the profiterole pastry filled with custard and topped with chocolate sauce— makes a most delicious dessert similar to eclairs but with far fewer calories and less fat, not to mention cholesterol.

PROFITEROLES
        Vegetable oil cooking spray
    1   cup water
    2¹/₂   tablespoons unsalted margarine
    ¹/₈   teaspoon salt
    2   teaspoons sugar
    1   cup all-purpose flour
        Thawed frozen egg substitute equal to 4 eggs

LIGHT CRÈME PÂTISSERIE
    2   tablespoons plus 1 teaspoon granulated sugar
    ¹/₂   cup thawed frozen egg substitute

2   tablespoons cornstarch
1   cup low fat (1%) milk
1   teaspoon vanilla extract

CHOCOLATE SAUCE
1   ounce semisweet chocolate
1¹/₂ tablespoons sugar
¹/₂   tablespoon cornstarch
¹/₄   cup low fat (1%) milk
¹/₂   cup evaporated low fat milk
1   teaspoon vanilla extract

1. Preheat oven to 400°F. Lightly coat a large baking sheet with cooking spray and set aside.

2. Combine water, margarine, salt, and sugar in a medium saucepan. Bring to a boil and let margarine melt (this will happen quickly). Adjust the heat to very low and add flour, beating with a wooden spoon. The dough will be very stiff. When mixture is combined and dough pulls away from the sides of the saucepan, remove pan from heat and stir in egg substitute, one quarter at a time, blending well after each addition. The dough should be thick, not runny.

3. Fit a pastry bag with a ¹/₂-inch plain tip and pipe 2-inch-diameter puffs onto the baking sheet, spaced at least 1 inch apart. If you don't have a pastry bag, drop generous tablespoonfuls of dough onto the cooking sheet.

4. Bake for 35 minutes or until puffed, crusty, and golden. While pastries bake, prepare the filling and sauce.

5. To prepare custard filling, combine sugar and egg substitute in a mixing bowl, then whisk in cornstarch. Heat milk in a small saucepan over a low flame to just below simmering. Stir ¹/₄ cup hot milk into egg mixture, then blend egg mixture back into saucepan. Cook over low heat, stirring

constantly, for 7 or 8 minutes or until custard is thick and glossy. Lift pot from the heat and stir in vanilla. Transfer mixture to a bowl, lay a piece of plastic wrap directly on the custard, and chill until pastry is ready to be filled.

6. To prepare sauce, heat chocolate on top of a double boiler. Stir in sugar and cornstarch and blend well, then add milks and extract and stir until smoothly blended. Turn off heat, cover, and keep warm (sauce can be refrigerated and gently reheated before serving).

7. Remove profiteroles from oven, pierce with a tooth-pick or thin skewer to let steam escape, and cool on a rack for 10 minutes. (If desired, the profiteroles can be frozen, whole, after they are cooled; reheat them in a 300°F. oven before cutting and serving.) If pastries are to be used right away, slit in half horizontally, remove any doughy centers, add custard filling, top with chocolate sauce, and serve.

MAKES 8 PROFITEROLES, 1 CUP FILLING, AND ¾ CUP SAUCE
APPROXIMATELY 108 CALORIES PER PROFITEROLE PASTRY
APPROXIMATELY 33 CALORIES PER 2 TABLESPOONS FILLING
APPROXIMATELY 47 CALORIES PER 1½ TABLESPOONS SAUCE

◆ ◆ ◆ ◆

APRICOT CRÈME

▶ ▶

Please bear in mind, any desserts made with whipped evaporated skim milk should be served within a few hours of preparation since the milk will eventually lose volume. However, the apricot puree can be prepared ahead of time and refrigerated.

This pale orange cream has a hint of tartness. Spoon it into goblets or long-stemmed wine glasses and top with sliced fresh strawberries.

1	cup evaporated skim milk
1/2	pound chopped dried apricot halves
2	cups water
1/4	cup plus 1 tablespoon sugar
1	tablespoon cornstarch
2	cups skim milk
3	tablespoons thawed frozen apple juice concentrate

1. Pour evaporated milk into a bowl and place bowl and beaters in freezer for 1 to 1½ hours or until a large rim of slush forms in bowl.

2. Meanwhile, combine apricot halves, water, and ¼ cup sugar in a medium saucepan and cook, stirring, for about 20 minutes or until apricots are soft.

3. Transfer apricot mixture to a food processor and process until smoothly pureed, or put through a food mill. Return to saucepan (you should have about 1½ cups puree. If you have more, press the puree through a sieve to extract some of the liquid).

4. Dissolve cornstarch in skim milk, add to apricot mixture and cook over low heat, stirring, until thickened. Add apple juice concentrate and stir to blend. Set aside to cool, then chill until cold (can be prepared 24 hours ahead).

5. Remove evaporated skim milk from freezer and whip with remaining sugar until peaks form. Fold into chilled apricot mixture just to blend and return to refrigerator to chill until serving time.

SERVES 8

APPROXIMATELY 171 CALORIES PER SERVING

◆ ◆ ◆ ◆

CHOLATE PUDDING PIE

▶ ▶

The crust and chocolate filling can both be made up to 24 hours in advance, but finish preparing this pie only a few hours ahead of serving.

1	cup evaporated skim milk
	Vegetable oil cooking spray
1¼	cups chocolate wafer crumbs (about 25 wafers)
2	tablespoons diet margarine, melted
2	cups low fat (1%) milk
¼	cup plus 2 tablespoons sugar
2	tablespoons cornstarch
4	tablespoons unsweetened cocoa
	Thawed frozen egg substitute equal to 2 eggs
2	teaspoons vanilla extract (1 teaspoon if using liqueur)
2	teaspoons hazelnut liqueur (optional)
½	ounce bittersweet chocolate, shaved
2	tablespoons finely chopped hazelnuts

1. Pour evaporated milk into a bowl and place bowl and beaters in freezer for 1 to 1½ hours or until a large rim of slush forms in bowl.

2. Preheat oven to 375°F. Lightly coat a 9-inch pie plate (I strongly recommend a nonstick pie plate for this type of crust) with cooking spray and set aside.

3. Combine wafer crumbs and margarine in a bowl. When well blended, press evenly onto the bottom and sides

of prepared pie plate, and bake for 8 minutes. Cool completely on a rack before filling (crust may be made ahead and refrigerated, covered).

4. In a medium saucepan, whisk together the low fat milk, 1/4 cup sugar, cornstarch, and cocoa. Cook, stirring constantly, over medium heat for 6 or 7 minutes or until mixture is very hot and begins to thicken.

5. Remove pan from heat and stir 1/4 cup hot milk mixture into the egg substitute, beating well, then add the egg mixture back into the saucepan. Add vanilla extract, and hazelnut liqueur if desired. Cook over very low heat, stirring, until thickened and glossy.

6. Transfer mixture to a bowl, press a piece of plastic wrap directly onto the filling, set bowl aside to cool, then refrigerate until cold (can be prepared 24 hours ahead).

7. Remove chocolate filling from refrigerator and beat at low speed of electric mixer just until creamy.

8. Remove evaporated milk from freezer and beat with remaining sugar until stiff. Fold whipped milk into chocolate filling and spoon into prepared crust. Garnish with shaved chocolate and hazelnuts and chill until serving time.

SERVES 8

APPROXIMATELY 227 CALORIES PER SERVING

◆ ◆ ◆ ◆

CARROT CRANBERRY
APPLESAUCE CAKE

▶ ▶

The name says it all. But you just can't imagine how
wonderfully well these fruits and carrots go together until
you try it. I confess, I sometimes eat it in the morning as
breakfast with my coffee, in the afternoon for lunch with a
scoop of low fat cottage cheese, or after a light dinner along
with a demitasse of espresso.

	Vegetable oil cooking spray
2¹/₂	cups all-purpose flour
1¹/₂	teaspoons baking powder
1¹/₂	teaspoons baking soda
¹/₂	teaspoon salt
1	teaspoon ground nutmeg
¹/₂	teaspoon ground cardamom
	Thawed frozen egg substitute equal to 4 eggs
¹/₃	cup sugar
2	tablespoons thawed frozen apple juice concentrate
2	teaspoons vanilla extract
¹/₄	cup vegetable oil
1¹/₂	cups Cranberry Applesauce (page 8)
3	cups finely shredded carrots

1. Preheat oven to 350°F. Lightly oil a 10-inch bundt
pan with cooking spray and dust with a tablespoon of flour,
tapping excess flour into a large bowl.

2. In the same bowl, sift together the remaining flour,
baking powder, baking soda, salt, nutmeg, and cardamom.

3. In a medium bowl, combine egg substitute with sugar, apple juice concentrate, and vanilla extract, mixing well. Add vegetable oil, cranberry applesauce, and carrots and blend.

4. Add wet ingredients to large bowl and mix just until flour is incorporated. Pour into prepared pan and bake 1 hour or until tester inserted all the way through comes out clean. Cool 10 minutes on rack, then invert cake onto a plate and cool completely.

SERVES 12
APPROXIMATELY 208 CALORIES PER SERVING

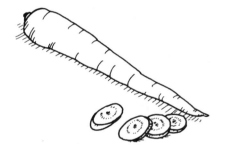

SUMMER FRUIT SOUP

▶ ▶

A delicious and unusual dessert, this dish also makes a good cold summer first course. Using fruit that is at the peak of freshness makes a difference here.

4	cups water
1	cup mildly sweet white wine, such as Sauternes
	Vanilla bean
	The peel of ½ large lemon, all white pith removed
1	thin slice ginger root (about the size of a quarter)
1	cinnamon stick
¼	cup fresh orange juice
1	tablespoon thawed frozen apple juice concentrate
1½	cups cubed fresh ripe pineapple
1	large ripe peach, peeled, pitted, and cubed
1	cup fresh blueberries, rinsed and chilled
	Four mint sprigs for garnish

1. Combine water, wine, vanilla bean, lemon peel, ginger, cinnamon stick, orange juice, and apple juice concentrate in a saucepan. Bring mixture to a boil, lower heat, and simmer about 10 minutes or until slightly reduced. Let mixture cool, strain and discard solids, cover, and chill thoroughly.

2. Just before serving, divide pineapple, peach, and blueberries among chilled soup plates. Pour chilled liquid over fruit. Garnish each plate with a mint sprig and serve cold.

SERVES 4

APPROXIMATELY 88 CALORIES PER SERVING

INDEX